GLÉNANS
GUIDES

YACHT HANDLING UNDER SAIL

Translated by Peter Davison

David & Charles

A David & Charles Book

Translation copyright © Peter Davison, 1995
First published in French as *Les Manoeuvres du Voilier*
Copyright © Éditions du Seuil, 1993
English translation, *Yacht Handling Under Sail*
first published 1995, ISBN 0 7153 0298 1

Peter Davison has asserted his right to be identified as
translator of this work in accordance with the Copyright, Designs and
Patents Act 1988.

Parts of this guide first appeared in
The Glénans Manual of Sailing, David & Charles 1993.
This book was prepared by Jean-Pierre Abraham,
Jean-Yves Béquignon and Jean-Louis Goldschmid,
with the help of Alain Malgoyre and the instructors'
committee at the Glénans sailing school. John Jameson
read and commented on the English translation.
Photographs: pages 20, 79, 85: Photothèque Glénans;
pages 7, 88: J.-L. Guéry/Neptune-Yachting;
page 31: Document Chantiers Janneau;
page 1: B. Stichelbaut/Glénans; page 55: P. Téqui.

A catalogue record of this book is available from the British Library

ISBN 0 7153 0298 1

Typeset by XL Publishing Services, Nairn
and printed in Italy by LEGO SpA
for David & Charles
Brunel House Newton Abbot Devon

C O N T E N T S

'Get out of that bunk! Come on, on with your oilskins, move outside and clip your harness on. It's your watch now, and time the boat calmed down so I can sleep.' Thus did I encourage the best crew I've ever had, Jean-Jacques Herbulot, to vacate his bunk for my weary frame. I wanted him to take the helm just as much as I wanted to lie down and shut my eyes. Inner peace is just as necessary for a good sleep as a snug sleeping-bag and a secure lee-cloth.

However lively the sea and wind, and whether it is day or night, your peace depends on a well chosen course and a sensitively steered boat. Get this right, and the rest is easy: sail trim, going about, cooking, sleeping. Even the stomach prone to seasickness is forgotten in the general harmony which engulfs your vessel.

The art of great sailors is no more, and no less, than this: to bring harmony to their vessels. It depends on mastering a few theories, cultivating one's intuition and knowing a myriad things about wind and water. But I cannot tell you which of these is most important. If you cannot tie the right knot, all your imaginative planning will be in vain. No crew can take in a reef unless they have learnt the tricks of the trade. And the best-intentioned helm will make everybody seasick if the boat is plunging up and down straight into a heavy swell.

*Y*ou approach perfection through a series of approximations, but you never quite get there... thank goodness. If perfection were attainable, what fun would there be in going to sea? We sail the oceans to enjoy that fabulous sense of freedom opening up before our bow; the words 'pleasure boat' take on a new resonance in such moments.

*F*reedom has its limits, on the ocean as elsewhere. The two most basic limits, I reckon, are the freedom of others and everyone's safety. The first of these depends on tolerance and mutual respect. The second, everyone's safety, depends on everyone's competence. Surely the most basic safety measure is carrying out manoeuvres competently, whether we are talking about tying a knot quickly, trimming the sails beautifully, balancing the helm, coiling the halyards or giving orders clearly.

*Y*acht handling is a vast subject. You can never hope to cover it completely. You can continue talking about it while your boat has been taken out of the water for the winter and the dust is settling on your boots. But while we can never hope to be definitive, you will seldom have a guide like Jean-Jacques. I therefore commend this small book to you, in the hope that somewhere in the world, some time, the off-watch crew will sleep all the sounder.

JEAN-LOUIS GOLDSCHMID
(GOLDO)
TECHNICAL DIRECTOR (RETIRED)
THE GLÉNANS SCHOOL

1

BOATHANDLING

Good boathandling depends vitally on how much attention you pay to the wind. This basic truth should be tattooed on the forehead of every sailor: the wind is your only valid reference point, and you will achieve nothing in sailing until you are in harmony with the wind.

This reference point, of course, changes constantly. If you try to extract maximum performance from your boat, you must face up to needing to readjust your perfect trim of a moment ago, and you must live with constantly changing reality. The best sailor is the one who first notices and adapts to a change in the wind strength or direction. There is no other secret to it (as far as we know).

Adapting to circumstances means, in essence, changing the sail trim, the boat balance and the way you steer.

Throughout this chapter we shall return to these three points as they relate to each point of sailing and every wind strength. In reality, of course, there is more to sailing well than the combining of these elements, but the *relationship* between them will be shown to be fundamental. Changing one aspect of a boat's trim alters all the others, and boat speed depends on the balance between the forces at work.

Analysing the various situations helps us not to produce ready-made answers, but to indicate the directions in which you should search. There is no precise standard by which you can say, at such and such a time that boat is perfectly trimmed. For that reason, though you might come to know your boat intimately, the only real yardstick you have is that of the boat next to you; by comparing, you can make progress, and this is no less true for those who have no desire to enter into competition afloat. You might also maintain a notebook of the way your boat performs in varying winds, on a variety of courses and in different wave conditions, or with different sail trim (using marked halyards and sheets).

We shall start by looking at sailing to windward. The boat is set up and tuned to windward, and it is also when sailing to windward that you will gain or lose the most by the degree of attention you pay to the wind. We shall examine the windward leg in some detail.

Sailing to windward

Finding the best course

The ideal close-hauled course

Sailing to windward, one has to trim the sails to close-hauled. There are degrees of closeness, however! A boat which luffs up from a beam reach finds itself first on a close reach, then on a close fetch, then close-hauled, then pinching. If you pinch any further, you find yourself unable to make headway without tacking, and you are said to be head to wind.

Our best windward course is that which the boat should take ideally when it needs to make ground to windward by tacking. We should at this point make the distinction between this and the simple fact of heading for a given point which happens to require a close-hauled course to reach it in one tack. The case we are concerned with involves tacking, and choosing a course not by reference to any specific fixed point, but by reference to the wind (which is of course constantly changing). One is therefore interested in taking advantage of the variation in the wind to gain ground to windward while keeping speed up, and effectively reducing the angle which constitutes the head-to-wind zone. This zone varies in size depending on the wind and the state of the sea, the number of hulls and the way you sail the boat. In general, a boat making an angle of 50° or so either side of the wind can be said to be making a good windward course.

Some narrower-

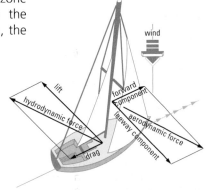

The force exerted on the sails by the wind (aerodynamic force) is at right angles to the sails, and is applied (simplifying slightly) at the centre of effort of the sail area. It can be broken down into a forward component parallel to the boat's axis, and a leeway component at right angles to the boat's axis.
When the boat is close-hauled, the leeway component is always much stronger than the forward component.
Hydrodynamic force (that of the water on the underwater surfaces) is applied more or less at the centre of lateral resistance of the hull; it will be equal and opposite to the aerodynamic force. It can be broken down into drag, parallel to the boat's axis, and lift, at right angles to it. The lift is equal and opposite to the leeway component.

■

Which wind?

1 True wind. This is the wind which is blowing over a given stretch of water, and which you can feel on your face when the boat is moored.

2 Relative wind. This is the wind created by the speed of the boat itself.

3 Apparent wind. This is the only wind you can actually feel (or use) while the boat is moving.

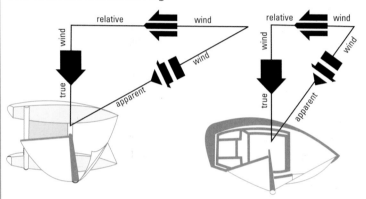

Catamarans have a higher relative wind because of their greater speed. The apparent wind therefore comes from further ahead, and the sails have to be sheeted more tightly.

The apparent wind is a combination of the true wind and the relative wind.

The apparent wind is always further ahead than the true wind; the difference between their angles of incidence is often as high as 20°, and can reach 60° on a reach.

The apparent wind is stronger than the true wind when the boat is close-hauled, and weaker when the boat is running. It can be as much as 80 per cent stronger or 50 per cent weaker. The difference can be noticed most strongly when you change course.

These differences in direction and strength are very marked on multihulls. These can be said to make their own wind, as they go faster and faster.

hulled boats can manage as little as 85° between tacks (the America's Cup yacht *Ville de Paris* could get as close as 40° to the wind!); but in a very strong or very light wind this can become 120°–140° in the same boat. (The best windward course can be made in moderate weather.)

Your ability to sail close to the wind is limited by the need to keep your speed up. When you are close-hauled, the force of the wind on the sails has a strong sideways component and heeling couple and a relatively weak forward component. The boat's leeway is only limited

11

by its speed, which provides lift over the keel. To keep your speed up, you cannot afford to sail too close to the wind.

The optimum close-hauled course is a compromise between heading and boat speed, and a battle against leeway.

Depending on the strength of the wind, the state of the sea and tactical considerations, one of the requirements may have higher pri-

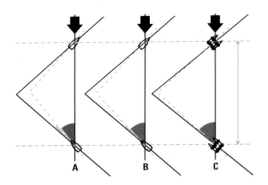

The dilemma: do you stick close to the wind to cut down the distance, or free off a little to sail faster? These three boats have taken three different routes but arrive together. Boat A has sailed the least distance.

ority than the others: you might pinch to reduce the overall distance sailed, at the risk of slowing down and increasing leeway; or you might sail slightly faster, further and freer, with less leeway.

For example, you might head at 45° to the wind, making 5 knots, with 5° of drift; if you were to head at 49° to the wind, making 5.25 knots and only 3° drift, you would only lose a total of 2°. Would this be offset by the extra speed? The problem is to know at what point the extra speed gained by sailing slightly freer is cancelled out by the extra distance to be covered. You can make a good comparison with other boats sailing the same course to experiment on this point; or you can even carry out the calculations if you have the necessary instruments on board. But you usually find out the answer in a race only at the windward mark.

There is unfortunately no general rule we can cite: any results will be valid only for the precise situation in which they were derived. The compromise between heading and speed is a constantly shifting one. Since conditions will always be changing, the search for your ideal is never-ending.

Almost close-hauled

Let us leave the lofty heights of theory and look at what happens on the water to a beginner trying to make the best course possible to windward.

Our novice crew in the first chapter set off from a reaching course, trimming the sails and gradually luffing up. We defined close-hauled as that point of sailing reached when the sails were completely pulled tight and to luff any further would cause them to flap.

The result of looking at it this way is often dreadful. The boat thuds into the waves, pinching hard, with its airflow restricted, making massive leeway. The beginner often sails in light to moderate winds with the sails in too tight and the boat pointed too high.

To get out of this position, work out:

■ the angle A of the sail to the wind: we know that the force exerted on the sail by the wind is due to the air being deflected, and is at a maximum for an angle of deflection of between 15° and 25°; the implication of this is that you should pull the sail in as hard as possible to reach this angle ;

■ the angle B of the sail to the boat: the force exerted by the wind on the sail is at right angles to the sail; thus, the less this is pulled in, the greater the forward component.

You will notice that the second consideration is a limiting factor on the first.

So what do you do?
The first thing to do is to ease the sheets a touch. You will feel the boat sigh with relief; it will drift less, even if it does not yet pick up much more speed. When you are close-hauled, it is difficult to get the boat to accelerate, even with perfect sail trim, once it has slowed down.

You therefore bear away slightly as well. Now you will feel the acceleration.

Once you have picked up speed, luff up a little again and try to find a good compromise between heading and boat speed.

The correct compromise is a series of approximations, as you adjust the sails to your course, and the course to the set of the

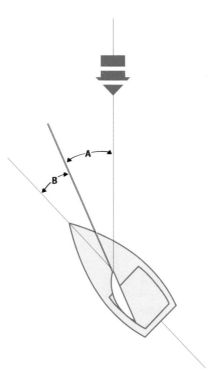

The dilemma viewed graphically: as you pull the sail in, angle A increases and so does the force exerted on the sail; as you ease the sail, angle B increases and so does the forward component of the thrust.

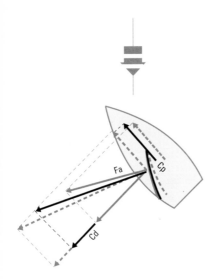

The sail trim shown in black is the best compromise: the aerodynamic force (Fa) is large and pointed fairly well forward, the propulsive component (Cp) quite respectable and the leeway, or drift component (Cd) modest.
The dotted sail is too hard in: although Fa has been increased, this only has the effect of increasing Cd.
The blue sail has been freed too far: both Fa and Cp are smaller. This trim is recommended only in strong winds, when the boat would otherwise heel excessively.

sails...the lighter and faster the boat, the more difficult it is to achieve this compromise.

Achieving optimum sail trim

Let us consider the effect of three different trims for a sail.

■ The dotted sail is very hard in, drawing all the way to the luff, exerting considerable force directed mostly sideways: the boat heels and makes leeway. This sail trim has no virtues.

■ The blue sail is very free, such that the luff is flapping. It exerts less force (the propulsive component is weaker), but the force is at least directed mostly forwards. This is not ideal, but we shall see that it has some advantages in a strong breeze when the heeling couple would otherwise be too strong for the boat and crew.

■ The best trim is clearly the middle one, in black. The force is almost as great as in the first instance, but there is noticeably less leeway. The sail luff quivers slightly, as it is trimmed until the sail 'lifts'.

Sailing the optimum course

The sail trims we have just considered all related to a single course; we also need to see whether the course itself can be improved.

When we look at the speed curve of a sailing dinghy on different headings (see page 16), we notice immediately that OA is the best close-hauled course but progress is almost as good on course OB. We have a certain amount of choice: there might be an ideal course, but courses a couple of degrees either side are not vastly different in terms of the progress to windward they permit. Thus one can vary the heading to suit the sea conditions and any tactical considerations. This freedom, however, only extends a few degrees either side of the ideal, and is reduced in strong winds or with a poorly trimmed boat.

Although you have achieved a compromise between course and sail trim, you cannot sit back and enjoy it. Even in a constant wind, your ideal compromise will be undermined by a number of factors.

Particularly at the beginning, you only need one mistake with the tiller to destroy the whole balance:

■ bearing away will cause the boat to speed up but will take you further from your destination;

■ sailing too close to the wind will bring you back to the first mistake we looked at: this mistake will be swiftly punished by your making less speed and more leeway.

We make no apologies for repeating this point: there is a chain reaction here which destroys the boat's momentum and can even leave it dangerously hard to control, if you are just to windward of the shore, for instance. The boat stops and drifts round as the flow of wind over the sails and the flow of water over the underwater surfaces stall. There is only one way out of this situation: admitting it has happened, freeing the sails to re-establish a smooth flow and bearing away to induce laminar flow over the centreboard. Only then, when you have regained sufficient way to steer, can you think about hardening back on to a close-hauled course, slowly, so as to pick up speed on the way. The central point of this is the need to pick up speed.

At this stage we shall venture a general recommendation: particularly in the early days, you should sail to windward in a series of gentle, short luffs. This is known as feathering; on the one hand, it ensures that you are not gradually bearing away without realising it, and on the other, it ensures that you do not miss any chances if the wind frees you to make a better course.

You cannot use the technique of feathering to sail a multihull to windward, as the apparent wind changes considerably with even a slight slowing of the boat.

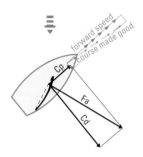

This is a good compromise. Despite a considerable drift component, the boat is not making excessive leeway.

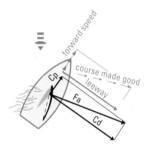

If you luff excessively, for instance to avoid an obstacle, the flow over the keel separates and the boat drifts sideways. If you then need to tack, you could find this is impossible because you have not got enough speed for the rudder to work. The only way out is to bear away drastically.

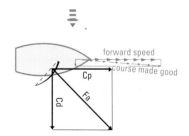

After bearing away radically, the boat has picked up enough speed and the drift has reduced sufficiently for the flow over the keel to become laminar again. Now you can luff up again.

15

All this is approximate. Sailing really well to windward is a skill which takes a long time to acquire. Sailing downwind, the consequences of a mistake are less severe, and differences between boats tend to be less marked; to windward, even boats of the same class will make noticeably different progress without any obvious reason. This shows that there is a certain skill involved in trimming the sails, steering and balancing the boat. It is time to go into detail on these topics.

Better than almost close-hauled

You need to draw a speed curve for different wind, sea and sail conditions, which will permit serious study of your close-hauled course.

Refer to the combined diagrams for a catamaran and a monohull. The sectors between A and B show the acceptable courses, with OA as the ideal course. The catamaran has a wider range of acceptable courses than the monohull. Its speed continues to pick up considerably further off the wind than OB.

How can you weigh the potential 10 per cent gain to windward of sailing OA against the extra 2 knots achieved by sailing OB? Monohulls are simpler, but studying the diagram is useful nevertheless.

Best of all, but most expensive is the on-board computer which can store all the data necessary to work out boat speed against angle to the wind. It can then suggest what it believes (on the basis of the information you have given it) to be the optimum course to sail in the conditions.

This expensive gadget is most worth while for a racing catamaran, where you are always travelling very fast, so that it is easy to forget that it might be possible to add another 10 per cent or so to your speed.

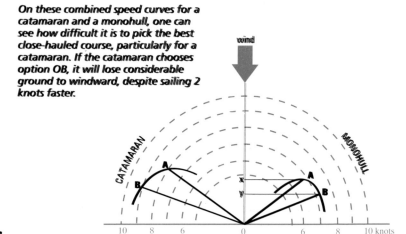

On these combined speed curves for a catamaran and a monohull, one can see how difficult it is to pick the best close-hauled course, particularly for a catamaran. If the catamaran chooses option OB, it will lose considerable ground to windward, despite sailing 2 knots faster.

Sail trim close-hauled

Sail shape

When you are sailing close-hauled, as we have seen, the sails need to be trimmed to the point where they lift. We can state this more precisely: the sails are correctly trimmed when the luff lifts slightly, simultaneously over its full length.

Achieving this ideal state means looking not only at the angle of the sails to the wind, but also at their shape. Shape and angle are closely related.

Camber

Controlling the camber of the sail is essential for windward sailing. Two properties of the camber need to be adjusted according to the strength of the wind:

■ its position. The maximum camber of the sail should always be at about the centre of the sail. When the wind freshens, the camber tends to move aft. It can be pulled forward (on the mainsail) by tightening the luff or (on the jib) by using the backstays or the runners to tighten the luff;

■ its depth. The stronger the wind, the flatter the sails need to be to reduce the deflection caused. You should bear in mind that *the reason for flattening the sails in strong winds is not so they can be sheeted tighter, but so they can be freed further before they start to flap.*

Twist

Sails have a greater or lesser tendency to twist, with the higher part of the sail (which is less controlled than the bottom) falling away under the wind. Although this tendency has to be controlled, it is not in itself a problem: the wind is stronger higher above the water (about 10 per cent stronger 10 metres up), so the apparent wind comes freer the higher up the sail you go. For this reason the sail can be sheeted in less tight at the top than lower down. As the aerodynamic force has a stronger forward component higher up, it creates less of a heeling couple.

The twist should be stronger still for a mainsail set aft of a jib, as the air lower down will already have

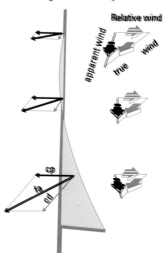

Since the true wind is stronger higher up the sail, the apparent wind is freer. A certain amount of twist in the sail gives you an aerodynamic force which is directed further forward, and a smaller heeling couple.

17

■

Using the mainsheet traveller

The mainsheet traveller is used basically when sailing close-hauled; if it is very long it can also be useful on other points of sailing. It allows you to control twist in the sail as you change sail angle. Playing the traveller either close to the centreline or down to leeward, you can ease or trim the sail without changing the tension on the sheet. You are opening or closing the slot by doing this. You can use the traveller to increase twist in the sail, bringing it slightly up to windward and letting the sheet out.

If you have a bendy rig, you can use the traveller to flatten the sail by bending the mast, without necessarily sheeting the sail in.

When you gybe, the traveller can slam from one end of its bar to the other and cause itself a fair amount of damage. It is a worthwhile precaution to centre the traveller when you are running, to avoid this problem.

■

Using the kicking strap

The kicking strap can be used when you are close-hauled, to control the twist in the sail if you have no traveller. It is used for this purpose on all boats when sailing off the wind, when the sail is too far out for the traveller to be of use. It also partly takes up the camber in the sail by helping to bend the mast.

been deflected by the jib, and if the twist were not there, the entire lower luff would be backwinded.

As the wind strengthens, you may find it useful to accentuate the twist, so as to reduce power up top and keep the heel under control.

For these reasons the mainsheet traveller needs to be brought towards the centre of the boat in light winds; if the traveller is cleated too far to leeward, you will find that the bottom of the sail is too free and the top too firmly sheeted.

We have already studied the reasons for needing to control sail shape; here we shall just quickly revise the means at your disposal.

Means of controlling jib shape
The degree of camber in a jib is generally invariable. When the wind changes in strength, you need to change jibs. In a few cases, you can control the camber by tightening the luff.

The twist can be controlled by moving the fairlead fore and aft, or by changing the height of the tack.

Means of controlling the mainsail

The position of the curve can be altered by luff tension; the degree of curve is determined by the foot tension and by the degree of bend you put in the mast by using the kicker, the mainsheet traveller and the backstays.

The twist can also be controlled by using the kicker and the traveller.

Trimming the sails

Armed with these new techniques, we are getting closer to a definition of close-hauled sail trim.

The jib is trimmed almost as far as it will go. The boat's course is then dependent on the jib: you head up until the luff lifts all the way up, then bear away by 2° or 3°.

The mainsail is sheeted in as little as possible, just enough for it not to be backwinded by the jib. The slot between the sails is then being made to work to its best effect.

The best sail trim is one in which both sails lift at the same time, from top to bottom of the luffs.

This is a question of cunning and subtlety, since the boat, to a large degree, makes its own wind. Particularly on a fast, light multihull, if you decide to feather into the wind just to check that you really are sailing as close to the wind as possible, you have a good chance of slowing the boat down, losing all that extra apparent wind and bringing the whole painstakingly achieved trim to nought. When this happens, there is nothing for it but to ease the sails and bear away, trimming them back in as the speed gets up, and so on…

Aids to correct sail trim

When there is a bit of a chop, the pitching of the boat tells you precisely whether the sails are correctly trimmed or not: well trimmed sails will lift slightly at the top when you are going down the back of a wave. This is caused by the top of the mast accelerating forward and causing a temporary increase in the relative wind, thus bringing the apparent wind further ahead. You know that you are too close to the wind if the sail is lifting constantly, and if it does not lift at all, you are sailing too free.

Tell-tales sewn on the sails can also be used (see page 20). The ones on the jib should be kept horizontal. If the jib is too tight, the leeward tell-tales will lift; and if it is much too tight they just hang limp. If the jib is excessively eased, the windward tell-tales are the ones which start to dance.

Tell-tales on the mainsail should stream out in the same direction as the sail; if it is sheeted too hard, they will fall off to leeward.

If not all the tell-tales react in the same way, you can tell that you have too much or too little twist in the sail.

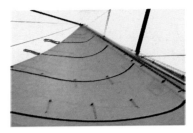

This mainsail is well set up, with the camber nicely situated and the tell-tales flying out straight.

This mainsail has the luff too slack, with the result that the camber has come aft and the sail has lost drive. The tell-tales dropping to leeward indicate that the sail is trimmed too tight.

The luff on this sail is too tight: the camber has been brought unnecessarily far forward.

Tell-tales and camber stripes

Coloured cloth stripes may be stuck or sewn on to the sail horizontally, a third of the way up and two-thirds of the way up. These can help you to see where on the sail the camber is and how deep it is. Tell-tales can also be attached to the leech of the mainsail to assist correct trim.

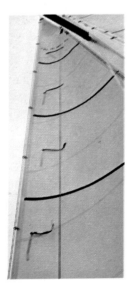

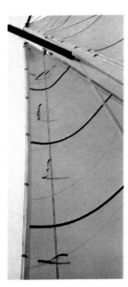

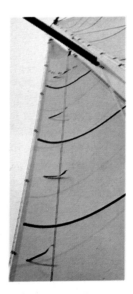

Jib sheeted much too tight, with the leeward tell-tales hanging down.

Jib eased too far, with windward tell-tales lifting.

Jib correctly trimmed, with both sets of tell-tales flying horizontal.

Boat trim

Sailing against the wind is almost unnatural, and the boat needs a lot of help to drive against the combined might of wind and waves. Balance and trim, lateral and longitudinal, are especially important.

Rudder balance

When a boat's sails are correctly trimmed and the tiller centred, yet the boat tends to luff up, it is said to have weather helm. Lee helm is the opposite. In either case, keeping the same course means using the tiller, which cuts speed, since the rudder acts as a brake when turned.

A boat's rudder balance is most critical when it is being sailed close-hauled; and it is most readily adjusted when close-hauled. A boat which is well tuned for the windward leg is usually set up correctly for other points of sailing as well.

The mast can be brought (or raked) forward to give less weather helm; the boat will have more weather helm if the mast is brought or raked aft. But moving the mast may have other effects and result in the opposite to what you are seeking. Only experimentation will tell.

The centreboard should theoretically be pushed right down for the windward leg to offset leeway which is strongest on this point of sailing. But, if the board pivots, you might find it useful to lift it just a touch, which will not reduce the surface but will bring the centre of lateral resistance aft and slightly change the balance of the boat. If you have two centreboards, only the leeward one need be used.

There are cases in which these theories must be treated with caution. The faster you travel, the more lift the centreboard creates, so you need less of the board in the water. Catamarans can quite confidently raise one centreboard when travelling above a certain speed.

You can choose which to raise depending on your aims: if your main concern is safety, raise the leeward board, so the boat will sideslip rather than heel; and if your aim is to sail fast, raise the windward plate, thus encouraging the early flying of the windward hull.

Should a boat be perfectly balanced to the helm, or should it have a little weather helm? There are a few who like lee helm, but these are rare birds. Certainly excessive helm pull in either direction is damaging. For beginners, we reckon a little weather helm is useful, as it keeps the boat feeling lively and responsive. A boat with a perfectly neutral helm requires a great deal of skill and concentration to sail well. In the end though, dinghy sailors can tune the boat to their own taste; but a cruiser which may be helmed by a number of people should definitely be set up with weather helm, since this gives a 'feel' which people become accustomed to more quickly.

Longitudinal trim

A boat will only sail well if she is floating on her designed waterline,

21

thus neither too light nor too heavy overall or at bow or stern.

In general, weight should be kept to the centre of the boat. It will pitch excessively in choppy water if there is too much weight toward the ends, and become quite uncomfortable.

These principles hold for all boats, large and small, heavy and light, but they are particularly important when the weight of the crew and equipment represent a large proportion of the total weight at that point – if, for instance, a member of the crew goes forward to the bow to change a sail, or someone is fishing from the aft pulpit, this increases pitching and slows the boat.

Lateral trim

A boat should be sailed as flat as possible. Once it starts to heel, the hull loses its designed underwater shape, and the boat is slowed. Heel also causes excessive weather helm in almost all boats.

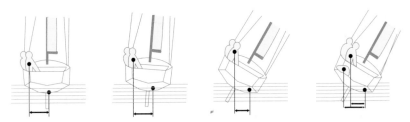

The righting couple of the crew weight increases when the boat starts to heel, but reduces as soon as the angle of heel increases further. Sleeping crew members below decks can make a significant difference.

Heel can be controlled by a combination of correct sail trim and the correct disposition of crew weight, usually by leaning out. There are two essential rules which apply:

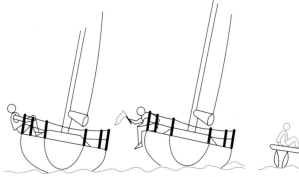 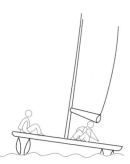

These two figures are helping to keep their respective boats flat. The person on the right is reminding the one on the left that it is forbidden to race with one's body outside the safety lines.

The optimum angle of heel of a catamaran is when one hull is just skimming the surface of the water.

Leaning out is very efficient when the boat is still almost flat, but its efficiency reduces considerably once the boat moves beyond a minimal angle of heel. A small amount of heel may occasionally be desirable, particularly in light winds, to keep the sails filled and reduce the wetted area.

Some narrow yachts are designed to be sailed heeled over, since this lengthens their waterline. These include the Dragon and 5.5m JI class.

Leaning out is more efficient the closer you are to the waterline. This is particularly true if boats are wide at the waterline, such as those with a hard chine: you can exert more righting moment by lying down quietly in your bunk than by clinging on grimly to the top edge of the deck.

Multihulls are so wide that any lateral crew movement has a considerable effect. You can exploit this fact in a catamaran to reduce the wetted area, by raising one hull just above the water. A few degrees of heel will give optimum power without destroying the efficiency of the underwater shape for the windward course.

How to steer

The basic principle to be followed is that the helm should not be used excessively or too suddenly. Speed is your vital weapon, so it should not be thrown away thoughtlessly; every twitch of the rudder reduces your speed slightly.

Beyond this fundamental rule, good steering is largely an intuitive matter which depends on your paying attention to everything that is going on. The experienced helm will feel the whole life of the boat through the tiller, especially if there is a touch of weather helm. When you are sailing close-hauled at a reasonable speed, you should find that the tiller becomes quite hard to move; and as you gain in experience, the sensation in the tiller can be used to give you all sorts of information about how the boat is sailing. The tiller moves more easily and has less 'feel' as the boat slows, and you know something is amiss.

The function of the tiller in a boat is similar to that of the reins for a horse: it must not be used to slow you down with excessive control, but to guide your steed to give its maximum performance in the desired direction. A well-tuned boat knows what it has to do. You need, in turn, to learn what the boat will do of its own accord and what you need to make it do. As you learn its habits and its limits, you will use the tiller less as a way out of trouble than as a way to avoid it in the first place.

Everyone has their own style and their own philosophy of steering. One of the chief variables, we suspect, is the captain's age.

The boat cannot be tuned in a day. You need practice together over a period of medium-strength winds (which is a rather vague expression, meaning something different for every boat and every crew, but which in effect implies that you do not need to go looking for the wind, but you are not suffering severe problems with excess heeling either).

You also need the practice wind to be constant, a still more questionable concept when applied to wind. We have maintained throughout this book that there is seldom such a thing as a wind which is constant in direction. To approach a feeling of what relative constancy might mean, we have to look more closely at its (very common) opposite: variability. We shall follow this up with a look at fresh and light winds.

Gusts

A temporary increase in wind speed is a gust, when the wind is otherwise light to medium in strength. An increase in an already strong wind we shall refer to as a squall. There is no clear boundary between the two: it depends on the size of the boat and the state of mind of the crew.

What happens in a gust?

The apparent wind, which is the one which fills your sails, is a combination of the true wind and the relative wind created by the speed of the boat. It comes from a direction between the two, which is therefore always further ahead than the true wind. The point to be noted here is that any change in strength of either of its component parts changes both the strength and the direction of the apparent wind.

The gust hits you.

Phase 1. The true wind increases in strength. The boat does not react immediately, so the relative wind remains the same. The direction of the apparent wind comes closer to that of the true wind, and you are freed.

Phase 2. The boat, sails correctly trimmed, accelerates. The relative wind increases in strength. The apparent wind heads you.

The gust passes.

Phase 3. The true wind subsides. The boat has momentum and does not slow down immediately, so the direction of the apparent wind moves even further ahead and you are headed still more.

Phase 4. The boat slows and the apparent wind returns to its original direction.

How does one react?

Particularly when you are close-hauled, a gust is an opportunity to make more ground to windward than the true wind would normally permit. In order to take advantage of the opportunity, you have to see it coming and immediately trim the boat correctly for the new wind.

On a small boat with quick reactions, you can luff and trim the sails in; for the mainsail, this usually means pulling the traveller in.

On a larger boat, with the sheets made off round winches, you will not have time to re-trim the sails, so you simply change your heading, by luffing up when the gust arrives, thus keeping the sails at the correct angle to the wind.

As soon as the relative wind component increases, you need to bear away so as not to let the sails flap and to maintain the extra momentum you have been given by the gust.

Of course, wind variations are not always this predictable, but the principle remains the same: keep an eye out to weather.

Strong winds

Strong winds usually make sailing less comfortable. In heavy weather the boat begins to heel excessively and becomes difficult to handle, when the movement of the hull through the water becomes difficult and landlubbers' faces turn green at the sight of the waves.

There is no way of making an ideal course to windward in heavy weather: with reduced lift from the sails, heavy wave motion and increased windage on the hull, it is more a question of limiting your boat's heel and finding ways of conserving its momentum.

Reducing the lift of the sails

As the wind freshens to a point where the weight of the crew and the natural tendency of the boat to sit flat in the water are not sufficient to keep it correctly trimmed, the sails need to be flattened and eased.

As the wind freshens, you need to reduce the angle through which it is deflected by the sails. This ensures that the aerodynamic force does not increase in the same proportion as the wind strength. Initially, this measure is sufficient on its own. The angle of deflection is reduced by flattening the sail and easing it out. The drawing (right) shows that by easing the sail (in black), you can increase the propulsive component Cp without an increase in Fa, the aerodynamic force.

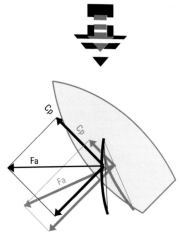

The apparent wind is a combination of the true wind and the relative wind. When the wind freshens, the sails need to be flattened. The total aerodynamic force does not increase, but the forward (propulsive) component does.

25

Trimming the mainsail

The camber of the mainsail is reduced and kept in the same place. The sail is then trimmed until it lifts, with the traveller fully to leeward. If you need to, you can increase the amount of twist in the sail by increasing mast bend with more backstay tension, until the head is not pulling at all. This will have the effect of reducing the heeling moment.

Trimming the jib

Before you trim the jib, you have to decide which one to rig for the wind. One can adjust certain jibs by stretching the luff, which flattens the jib somewhat and prevents the camber from moving aft. This is an essential feature for furling jibs. Using a flatter, heavier jib is a better solution.

So as to stop the jib losing its shape, you need the forestay to be as tight as possible. A slack forestay sags to leeward, causing the sail to belly out and the camber to move aft, while the leech tightens and closes the slot. At this stage the jib is not pulling the boat forward at all: it is just heeling the boat.

It is also possible to let the head of the jib twist: if you bring the sheet fairlead aft or up, this will tension the foot and slacken the leech.

The interaction of the sails: the 'slot'

The jib can tend to backwind the main. If this happens, it is usually because the jib has too much camber. It then needs either to be flattened or to be changed.

When the jib has been flattened and trimmed as much as possible and is still backwinding the main, it is better to let the main luff lift than to pull it in any further and kill any boat speed you might otherwise pick up.

In strong winds, the boat is correctly tuned when both sails lift at the same time, on the top half only. This way you can reduce the power in the sails by a small luff.

If the boat has a bendy mast, like many dinghies, the same result can be achieved using the various mast bend controls.

Reducing sail

If the wind freshens still more, these techniques will be insufficient, and you have to think about actually reducing the sail area. This will be done earlier on some boats than on others, and to a varying degree.

The first reef is intended primarily to take up most of the luff curvature.

First reef

The first reef will certainly reduce the area of the mainsail, but above all it will absorb the curvature of the luff of the sail, taking up most of the fullness. The main function of the first reef is to flatten the sail. For this reason the first reef is usually smaller than the others, and is sometimes called a flattening reef. The first change of headsail is often to a smaller and certainly flatter jib.

Second reef

When cutting the power by flattening the sail is no longer enough, you have to start cutting the surface area. Two or three reefs can be taken in a mainsail, and the jibs become successively smaller, and cut to accommodate increased forestay sag. With a furling jib, roll up until heeling is reduced to an acceptable angle.

Balancing the sails

As you reduce the sail area fore and aft, your main aim is not to unbalance the boat. Do not be misled by the fact that a boat develops weather helm when it heels, into the mistake of compensating by leaving too much sail up forward.

Let us look at a typical example.

Two Sélections (five tonners which have weather helm when they heel) are sailing together in the Western Channel in a wind freshening to force 8.

One of them reduces its sail area regularly as the wind increases, fore and aft, so that soon it has only a storm jib and the mainsail down to the last reef. With both sails sheeted tight but the mainsheet traveller fully eased, this boat will be sailing well on a close fetch.

The skipper of the other is concerned to ensure that the boat does not develop weather helm, so keeps a fair-sized jib up as long as possible. As the wind freshens, this boat makes each change a little later than the other: thus, the number 1 jib is hoisted when the other has its number 2 up, and the number 2 is only hoisted when the other has already resorted to the storm jib. On the other hand, this boat treats the mainsail with caution and takes in a reef one stage earlier than our first boat.

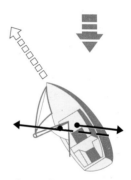

The reef is in place with the main flattened and a suitably sized jib hoisted: the boat is nicely balanced.

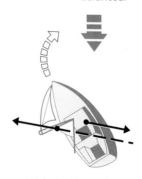

With the jib too large and too full, the boat will heel excessively and develop a lot of weather helm, despite the fact that the mainsail area has been reduced.

27

Finally, as the boat continues to heel alarmingly, they are left with the number 2 jib, and no mainsail up at all. The boat is still heeling badly and still has weather helm; the jib is too full for the weather conditions and the forestay sags : this boat is going nowhere fast.

This instance gives us a further principle to follow when choosing sails in fresh weather: to keep the boat balanced, you need to pay as much attention to the shape of the sails as to their surface area.

Balancing the boat

A boat can still heel considerably under reduced sail, and it is worth repeating that your aim should still be to sail it as flat as possible.

A smaller cruiser such as a Glénans 7.60 or the Tonic 23, with a stable hull form, can be kept driving in winds up to force 7 or 8, just so long as it is sailed as flat as possible, with flattened sails, which are eased as the occasion demands.

Working the waves

Even if the boat is sailed with a good fore-and-aft trim, it will find that the waves begin to cause problems as the wind gets up. This is especially the case with lighter boats and multihulls.

Heavy cruisers

The heavier the boat, the more momentum it has, and consequently the less it is affected by this problem.

There are two ways of dealing with the waves to windward:

1 Sailing up the side of the wave at a slight slant, then luffing as soon as the crest of the wave passes; if the waves are coming from the same direction as the wind, you will probably find that the boat does this of its own accord.

2 Luffing and sailing straight up the slope of the wave, then bearing away down the back of the wave to regain speed; this is usually the only way to cope with waves which are coming straight at you, from further ahead than the wind.

When the waves are breaking, you have no choice: you must take them bow on, even if this slows the boat considerably. (This recommendation is slightly optimistic, as a wind strong enough to cause breakers out at sea is likely to be too strong for you to luff up under perfect control at will.)

Even with a heavy boat, your prime aim must be to keep the boat's momentum up, simply as a safety precaution. If you feel the boat slowing too much, bear away and keep your speed up rather than sticking to your heading and letting the boat lose way.

Light cruisers

A light cruiser has much more difficulty in waves: the dilemma is that the boat will be severely slowed if it crashes into the waves, and it will also be severely slowed if its sails stop drawing.

The aim, then, must be to steer up the side of the waves without losing the wind from the sails.

The procedure should be as follows:

■ at the top of a wave, the relative wind is noticeably stronger, so the apparent wind shifts further ahead; you need to bear away to keep the sails drawing;

■ at the bottom of the wave, with less relative wind, you are freed and can afford to luff up.

In fact this only works in a sea which is moderately rough and a wind which is moderately strong. As the waves and wind build up more, things change: between waves, you might not even have any wind in the bottom half of your sails, and you need to respond as follows:

■ bear away in the hollows, so as to keep the top of your sails (which is the only part with wind) drawing;

■ luff hard at the crest of the waves so the boat does not heel too badly.

You will see that the two techniques are exactly opposite, and you will quickly notice which is the appropriate method for the wind and sea conditions you are in. The principle of both is that you keep the sails drawing, to gather as much forward force as possible and prevent the boat being stopped in its tracks by the waves.

Catamarans

If you are flying a hull (which you will not be doing often on a cruise!) or if both hulls meet the wave together (probably equally rare), the techniques to use are the same as for the light cruiser. The reality is much more likely to be that the windward hull hits the wave before the leeward one does. The windward hull is then lifted up by the wave, and the crew begins to think that the boat is heeling and flying a hull, though it is in fact still sitting on the water. At this point, you need to luff in anticipation of the second hull hitting the wave and the boat being brought back level. The technique is therefore very similar to what you would do if you were working the wave with only the leeward hull to think about – it just feels rather different.

This situation, in which you are forced to luff, should not be confused with the situation which arises when one hull leaves the water because the boat is overpowered. If that happens, you should not luff at all, as that could well lead to a capsize.

In practice, one only has to work the waves in a catamaran if they are very steep. In any other case you just let the bows cut through them as you fly on!

Squalls

On a heavy cruiser it is best to use sails for the average wind force, so that you can survive the squalls without being flattened, but still make progress in the calm patches.

A reasonable compromise is to have a fairly flat jib that works well in the heavy gusts, and a rather fuller main which is of little use in the squalls but gives you a fair amount of power in the calms. The jib is left sheeted in during the squall, and the boat luffs, with the main freed off if necessary to stop the boat heeling further. When the wind drops, the main is sheeted back in and you bear away. With a bendy rig, you may not need to change course: the backstay is tensioned in the squall to open the top of the sail, and is let off again when the wind drops.

On a light cruiser sailing in squalls can be rather demanding: you need to be on your toes constantly to keep the boat moving.

Some people reckon that you should keep the jib sheeted in through the squall to maintain power, with the mainsheet eased as necessary to keep the boat flat, while the crew sits as hard out to windward as possible.

This can have undesirable effects, however: the mainsail can become fuller when the sheet is eased; so too can the jib, if the forestay is anything other than very tight. In the end you can make the boat harder to control rather than easier.

There are two ways of avoiding this problem:

1 Luffing, rather than easing the mainsheet, so that the sails almost completely stop drawing. You must carry out this manoeuvre with a great deal of skill and precision if you are going to do it: you should aim to respond to the strength of the squall as it passes, keeping the boat flat but moving,

2 Easing the traveller rather than the sheet, so that the sail keeps the boat moving forward without excessive heel, and remains flat.

You are likely to need to apply both these solutions in practice.

On a catamaran the second of the above solutions is almost certainly going to be the most effective measure you can adopt: the mainsheet traveller is long enough and the mainsail sufficiently big for it to become a much more effective weapon than it ever can be on a monohull. The procedure, then, in the following order, is:

■ mainsheet traveller down to leeward;
■ mainsheet eased;
■ jib sheet eased.

This only works if you react quickly to the squall.

Your reactions will be speeded up if you are holding the sheets throughout. If this is too demanding, you should have the quick-release mechanism in your hand instead.

Admittedly, the main could do with being freed off a little, but the sails are full, the boat slightly heeled… and you have the suspicion of a wake.

Light weather

We pass now to the gentle breeze that you can barely feel on your cheek. The first problem is telling exactly where the wind is coming from. Cigarette smoke is most effective. An alternative is to take your shirt off and see where the first goose pimples appear… Quite frequently, in fact, there may be no wind down where you are sitting, but a little way up there will be enough breeze to stir the tell-tales or the burgee.

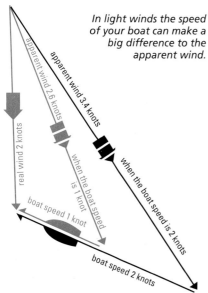

In light winds the speed of your boat can make a big difference to the apparent wind.

apparent wind 3.4 knots

apparent wind 2.6 knots

real wind 2 knots

when the boat speed is 1 knot

when the boat speed is 2 knots

boat speed 1 knot

boat speed 2 knots

A real close-hauled course is impossible in these conditions, as the resistance of the water on the hull is greater than the forward component of the thrust on the sails. You need to bear away if you are to gain any speed.

Sail trim

Since there is so little wind, it needs the greatest possible deflection, so you need the sails to be very full, and eased as far out as possible to bring their force well forward.

The sea will tend to be calm in light airs, though there can still be a swell; the

31

regular flapping of the sails caused by the rolling motion of the waves can be harnessed and used to your advantage. Light airs can be a real test of crew and boat.

Boat trim

The crew sits well inside the boat to reduce windage. If you sit rather further forward than usual, this will pick the transom out of the water and also give a touch of weather helm. The boat should be slightly heeled to reduce the wetted area and keep the sails filling on the right side. Any abrupt movement should be avoided. You have at all costs to maintain your momentum.

Steering

The tiller needs to be handled with extreme care. More than ever, sudden changes in direction must be avoided.

If you pinch into the wind, you will feel the boat slow down immediately. Since your own relative wind was contributing a significant part of the total apparent wind, this is serious. You need to bear away and ease the sails considerably to pick up speed again.

If you bear away too far, you will 'stall' the sails. At this point the boat will slow and the wind will seem to have left you for ever. Ease the sails out, then luff back up again on to your course gently, bringing the sails in tighter as you go.

In light airs, every manoeuvre takes time, and mistakes take a very long time to put right.

Variable light airs

The slightest puff of wind is a treasure. You need to take from it everything you can get, without being hasty. When a puff hits you, since your sails are very full, you can sheet in and luff at the same time, thus gaining speed as well as ground to windward. But you must not try to stick to this new course: you should bear away as soon as the wind drops again, to keep whatever speed you have. Paradoxically, the boat's own relative wind is playing a major role in propelling it forward.

To make decent progress to windward in a light breeze is largely a matter of feel. It is a question of finding a point of sailing at which the wind feels strongest. When you achieve that, you know you are making the best windward progress you can.

Close fetching

The close fetch is that comfortable point just off the wind from close-hauled, at which the sails are full and drawing hard.

Trimming the boat for a close fetch is not all that different from trimming it for the close-hauled leg, but it will feel quite different.

You no longer need to worry about playing games with the fickle wind to get to some point in the dead zone to windward of you: from now on you have a fixed point to sail at and you can head directly for that point without difficulty.

Sail trim

The sails will be fuller and sheeted less tight than on the beat. Your aim on a close fetch should be to deflect the wind through as large an angle as possible while minimising the side-ways component of the force gener-ated. For this reason you should not ease the sheets as much as you might suppose from the change of heading.

When the wind freshens, you will not always need to flatten the sails. This depends to some extent on the sort of boat you are sailing: while some small boats cannot carry very full sails on a close fetch, this is less of a problem on heavy or large boats.

Steering

One's aim should be to stick to the desired course, changing the sail trim as necessary according to the varia-tions in wind strength and direction.

It is usually easy to maintain a steady course when close fetching. The boat is stable and easily controll-ed; for this reason the close fetch is the recommended point of approach to any manoeuvre which requires great precision, such as coming into a narrow channel, moving around a crowded harbour or coming up to the jetty. It is also a catamaran's best point of sailing: you will always find that the ideal windward course of a catamaran is less close to the wind than that of a monohull.

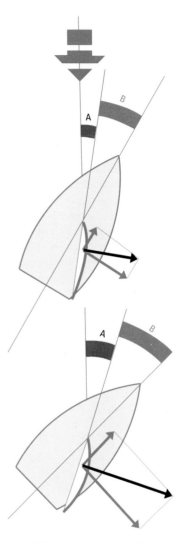

When you bear away from a beat on to a close fetch, the angle of deflection A increases to reach its optimum, of about 20°–25°. Rather than easing the sheets you should aim to increase the fullness in the sails.

Sailing to windward: summary

We should just explain one piece of terminology which will come up again and over which there should be no confusion: by 'sailing to windward' we mean sailing on any course which takes the boat upwind of where it started.

It follows that this point of sailing will be characterised by a certain set of the rig. For most monohulls, the act of sheeting the sails in close is synonymous with sailing to windward. However, light boats and particularly multihulls derive such a high proportion of their power from relative wind, which they effectively generate themselves, that we need to distinguish the sail trim from the course sailed. The faster the boat, the more significant this relative wind is as a proportion of the apparent wind which powers the sails. Since, by definition, the relative wind always comes from straight ahead, the apparent wind always comes from further ahead than the true wind. The practical consequence of this is that the sails of a cat may be trimmed as if close-hauled, all the way through to a beam or even a broad reach.

We started out by defining the ideal course to windward as a compromise between speed and course; ever since, we have been insisting on the need to maintain boat speed. Without speed there is no course. Speed, in the final analysis, has to be considered the prime concern of the windward leg. The boat needs to remain easy through the water, and consequently needs to be left a certain margin as it steers that narrow groove along the side of the 'dead zone'.

Downwind

In theory, sailing downwind is sailing with the wind directly behind the boat at 180°. In reality, this would be an extremely difficult course to sail for any length of time. We therefore define 'downwind' sailing as being in that sector which is 30° either side of dead downwind, and we therefore include a broad reach in this section.

In a moderate wind, running and broad reaching are extremely comfortable points of sailing. There are no complicated sums to work out and no particularly difficult strategic considerations: the wind pushes, the boat moves whether the sails are trimmed or not (in fact, whether the sails are hoisted or not!). You do not need any great speed to maintain your course, as there is no leeway. There are no problems with heeling. You can sit there and design magnificent spinnakers in your mind, as you sit there pleasantly at your ease. The boat runs with the waves rather than bashing into them. There is little apparent wind and the world is in harmony.

There is treachery afoot: the wind flatters to deceive. As soon as the wind freshens, all those charms seem a little less certain. The boat is still not slowed at all by the waves, and its carefree progress becomes a headlong rush, requiring every ounce of your concentration to keep it on course. Dangers beckon either side of the thin line you are sailing: one side of the road is marked 'gybe' and the other 'broach'.

Sail trim

Downwind, you will be showing off the full contents of your sail locker: mainsail, spinnaker, possibly a big boy and a few further exotica… if you are confident that you can use all these without getting into a muddle.

Mainsail

Off the wind, the airflow over the sails is non-laminar: it swirls around, and so the mainsail lacks power. To maximise its potential, you need to put shape into the mainsail, limit its twist and offer the maximum possible surface to the wind.

The mainsail works downwind through drag rather than lift. For the first time, your aim will be to maximise drag!

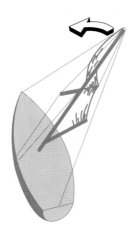

Twist in the sail is harmful downwind: the aerodynamic force on the top part of the sail acts in the wrong direction and heels the boat to windward. Here, the kicking strap needs tensioning.

Camber and twist

You can slacken the luff and the foot of the main, and even straighten the mast to increase the camber.

Use the kicking strap to reduce the amount of twist in the sail. Off the wind, there is no particular reason to have the head of the sail fall away to leeward; in fact, quite the contrary, since twist in the sail will encourage luffing and heeling to windward (bearing away) at the same time. This in turn can set up rhythmic rolling which makes it difficult to keep to your course.

Trim

Ideally, the mainsail should be at right angles to the wind, i.e. let out as far as it will go. There are a number of reasons not to go quite that far, however. For a start, the less sideways force there is on the sail from the wind, the more easily the boat will roll. Secondly, a fully eased main has the effect of disturbing the air flow around the spinnaker. And the final consideration has to be that if you let the main out all the way, it has a good chance of ruining itself by rubbing constantly against the shrouds.

35

Beware of the accidental gybe: make sure there is a figure-of-eight knot in the sheet to stop the boom hitting a shroud if it is whipped across; cleat the mainsheet traveller in the middle; and ease the runners if you have them (since there is no reason to tension the forestay when you are on a run).

Spinnaker
Downwind, the spinnaker is usually hoisted.

Just like other sails, the spinnaker is there to deflect the wind; because of its round shape it can deflect the wind through a very acute angle. The spinnaker is trimmed so as to get the air circulating as much as possible, which means that it needs to be set well forward and to windward so as to keep it away from the other sails. For this reason, you need to:

■ *Open the spinnaker up to windward* by poling it out so that the spinnaker pole is at right angles to the apparent wind. If the pole also travels round so it is at right angles to the boat's centreline, you know that you are sailing dead downwind. This is harder to achieve than it sounds, and you have to keep a certain scepticism about the wind you can actually feel down at deck level; it is better to put your faith in what the burgee is telling you, or (in light winds) to have a little tell-tale fixed to the middle of the spinnaker pole. It is fairly rare to manage to get the spinnaker pole exactly at right angles to the wind: in general, sea and wind conditions plus the predispositions of the boat and crew combine to move the pole as much as 10° or 15° from this 'ideal'. If you pull the pole to windward, you increase the lee helm, and if you let it drop to leeward, you increase the weather helm.

If you sheet the mainsail in slightly, air flows into and around the spinnaker better; since the forces acting on the two sails are in slightly different directions, the combination gives the boat some sideways 'grip' and prevents it rolling.

■ *Make the spinnaker fuller* by letting the foot rise up as high as possible, especially in light winds; this in turn may mean rigging it with very light sheets, or the clew will not rise enough.

The spinnaker should be *symmetrical around a vertical axis* (note, this really means plumb vertical, as opposed to the line of the mast). The foot should therefore be *horizontal*. The clew which is free can only rise up if the tack goes first. Thus, the pole has to be raised, and the clew will follow; if you raise the pole too far, the clew will flop back down and will have to be fished back up again by dropping the tack and starting anew.

On monohulls where it is possible to adjust the inboard pole height, the pole needs to be kept at right angles to the mast to avoid wear in the uphaul-downhaul system. It is not always possible to trim the pole this way on small cruisers, and the pole has to be allowed to rise slightly.

■ *Ease the sheet as much as possible.* Of course, this is how all the sails should be trimmed, but it is particularly important with the spinnaker, which *loses power unless it can empty itself of the air it has deflected.* A spinnaker which is sheeted in too hard traps the air and will collapse from the middle, wrapping itself firmly and affectionately round the forestay.

Whatever else you do, you should not sheet the spinnaker so tight that the foot touches the forestay.

Like other sails, spinnakers should be eased until they just lift. When a spinnaker is well trimmed, you will see a faint crease along the luff. This crease is not problematic in itself, but it tells you the spinnaker has been eased to its optimum point and will collapse if it goes out any further (not from the middle, in this case, but starting at the luff). A collapse can be quite sudden and upset the trim of the whole rig.

For this reason it is best to sail with the merest flutter in the luff rather than a noticeable crease.

Trimming the spinnaker

You cannot hope to trim the spinnaker and then leave it there. It is always precariously balanced, and can be knocked off balance by the boat rolling or any slight 'hole' in the wind.

While the spinnaker is up, therefore, one crew member will be exclusively dedicated to its care and trim, playing it constantly.

Adjusting the uphaul

Logically, you would expect to have to trim the sheet every time the spinnaker loses power, like any other sail. However, finesse in spinnaker trimming includes attention to the uphaul control. As we saw above, the spinnaker needs to be kept symmetrical about the vertical axis; failure to do so is the main cause of its

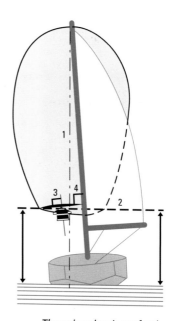

The spinnaker is perfectly trimmed when
1. it is vertically symmetrical;
2. the foot is horizontal;
3. the pole is perpendicular to the apparent wind...
4....and perpendicular to the mast as well.

37

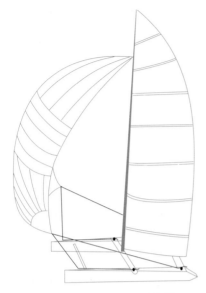

The spinnaker on a multihull. Catamarans are usually wide enough to allow a spinnaker to be used without a pole, which simplifies life, especially when gybing! With the sheet, guy and downhaul set, the sail can then be trimmed as on a monohull, except that you will not have to contend with the boat rolling or suddenly broaching. Yet another good reason to swap your monohull for a cat!

collapse. Incorrect trimming at the sheet will have the same effect but much later. Thus uphaul adjustment is critical in balancing the sail consistently; once you have achieved a balance, the pole can then be held in place by also tightening the downhaul. Do not forget that the clew will flop down just as readily if the tack is too high as if it is too low.

Just as you need to keep a constant eye on the uphaul, you need to watch out that your angle to the wind has not changed; the tell-tale on the spinnaker pole will usually be the first indicator of a change in wind direction (or of the helm not paying attention). If you stray seriously from your course, the spinnaker itself will alert you to the fact, by flapping if you have luffed up or by collapsing if you have borne away too far.

Trimming the sheet
Some people prefer to use the sheet to trim the spinnaker. If the

■

Spinnakers without tears, part 1

A: Spinnaker sheeted too hard, collapsing from the middle, just about to wrap itself round the forestay.
B: Spinnaker trimmed correctly, with a faint curl appearing at the top of the luff.
C: Spinnaker insufficiently sheeted, on the verge of a major collapse starting from the luff.

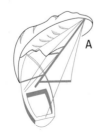
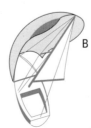
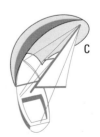

luff starts to fold, you need to grab an armful of sheet then let it go again once the sail fills; and if it starts to collapse from the centre, you have to ease the sheet rapidly. The tack height is adjusted afterwards: upwards if the luff folds high up, and downwards if the fold is close to the foot.

Off the wind on a multihull, one can generally do without a spinnaker pole, which is a relief. So long as the sheet and guy are trimmed symmetrically, the spinnaker should take shape naturally.

Other sails

Once you have trimmed the spinnaker successfully, why take the chance of wrecking that fragile balance by adding yet another sail? Why not? Logically, it must be possible to find more power somewhere… If you take a good look, there are still gaps in your rigging, where the air is slipping through without being put to work. Are you going to let this continue? There are at least two obvious places to catch more of the available air: one is underneath the spinnaker, where a spinnaker staysail can be set; the other, more important, gap is opposite the spinnaker, to leeward but away from the mainsail, where a very useful sail can be set in any wind of over 10 knots: the big boy.

The big boy is a sort of loose genoa, made of spinnaker cloth, with the clew high up, the foot longer than the leech and a heavily cutaway luff so that the sail sags well downwind of the spinnaker.

The sail is set 'flying'. It is shackled on to the stem and hoisted downwind of the spinnaker sheet, with a fairly slack halyard, the halyard sheave maybe 30 per cent of the mast height up. The foot should be set down by the surface of the water and the sheet fairlead should be as far aft as possible.

The big boy fills in the opposite direction from a genoa: the air enters at the leech and leaves via the luff. It follows that when the sail flaps it needs to be eased; at the same time the halyard needs to be tightened or the sail will droop in the water. When it stops flapping, you can sheet in a little again and let off the halyard. As you will appreciate, one member of the crew needs to be assigned permanently to the halyard.

The big boy gives the boat considerable stability, as it joins the area of the mainsail and more or less balances out the area of the spinnaker on the opposite side. The big boy will allow you to sail as far as 15° by the lee (though if you are doing this you should also rig a boom preventer). It will function under normal conditions as far as 40° from dead downwind. The trick is to make sure you always leave a sizeable slot between the spinnaker and the big boy to let the air escape freely. The spinnaker boom has to be rigged very square to allow this.

If you do not have a big boy, you can get away with a suitably cut

39

genoa (so long as the luff is not weighed down with hanks). In order to let enough air into the genoa, you will have to take a reef or two in the main.

Jib

Occasionally there will be too much wind for you to hoist the spinnaker. At this point you will have to make do with the jib.

You can pole a reasonably large genoa out to windward on the run, with the main reefed to the same size as it would be on a beat in the same wind (or perhaps a little larger). If there is a heavy swell, you must bear in mind the possibility of the pole catching a wave; to avoid this, use a smaller genoa or at least one with the clew cut higher. On the run, you can complete the picture with a big boy... but then again the boat is probably already virtually flat out, so the big boy might not help much.

If you are sailing too close for the genoa to pull when it is goosewinged, you can choose either to bear away a little to help it draw properly, or to harden up and set it in its usual position, to leeward. You have to decide how much of a hurry you are in.

We are not trying to push you into hurtling around at breakneck speeds, far from it! If you are at all nervous of the ideas presented, it is perfectly acceptable, and very safe, to sail downwind under jib alone, or with two jibs of which one or both are loose-luffed. If you do use two jibs, make sure there is a good gap left between them so the air can flow through.

Twin staysails

There is good reading matter to be found in sailors' tales featuring long days spent with a favourable trade wind across the Atlantic. If you are not obsessed by speed, twin jibs or twin staysails are a wonderful way of profiting from a constant wind from behind.

You need to use two spinnaker poles, preferably the telescopic sort. You will not need the mainsail: since the centre of effort is well forward, the boat has immense directional stability, and the autopilot (or just the piece of shock-cord attached to the helm) works at its best.

There is a more modern version of the twin-staysail arrangement, known as the booster. This is a double jib made of spinnaker cloth with a central luff tape; it does have an alternative use, as a very full jib, doubled over. It has to be said that this sail is designed for peace of mind and tranquillity, rather than high performance.

One note of caution on these long downwind stretches: if you have no mainsail up, it can take ages to get back to any crew member who falls overboard. Clunk click on the safety harness is greatly preferable to the sickening splash of the first mate's belly-flop.

Boat trim

Downwind, the boat's balance to the helm is dependent on the asymmetry of the sails as they are set:

■ with the mainsail well eased, and no other sail up, the boat tends naturally to luff up;

■ with a jib drawing to windward (i.e. the boat goosewinged), you can balance the helm by heeling the boat slightly to windward;

■ the spinnaker offsets the imbalance from the main more or less completely, but it can make monohulls heel to windward, giving an uncomfortable degree of lee helm.

In pleasant weather, without much of a sea running, the boat holds its heading easily. You can prevent broaches, as the fold in the spinnaker luff will warn you they are coming. It is of course less easy to spot a lurch to leeward approaching.

If you bear away a touch beyond dead downwind, so that you are by the lee, the spinnaker can have its wind stolen by the mainsail; it will then instantly collapse and wrap itself round the forestay in a wineglass shape. Once it starts, there is no stopping it. Luffing up just makes matters worse. To unwrap the spinnaker, you have to go through the whole procedure back-to-front, by gybing and sailing by the lee on the opposite tack. This usually makes the spinnaker unwrap itself without your further intervention.

As a general principle, in a monohull, it is better for the helm to luff up when something goes wrong under spinnaker than to bear

■

Spinnakers without tears, part 2

A: Either the spinnaker was sheeted in too tight or the helm has borne away too far and the boat is sailing by the lee...

B:...leading to this.

C: You therefore gybe the mainsail and rig a boom preventer.

D: Next bear away again so that you are sailing by the lee on the new tack, and the spinnaker unfurls of its own accord.

E: You can now gybe back on to the original tack and sail as you were before, trimming the guy and (most importantly) easing the sheet. Problem solved!

A   B   C   D   E

away; it is easier to bring a flapping spinnaker back under control than one which is wrapped around the forestay. However, even this reflex needs to be controlled, and not too violent: 10° or 15°, no more, or your luff can turn into an uncontrolled broach... A multihull must under no circumstances be allowed to heel uncontrollably, and there is in any case less chance of wrapping the spinnaker around the forestay, since the boat rolls less. For this reason, it is better to keep the wind behind you, even going so far as to gybe if necessary.

The centreboard

The centreboard is theoretically of little use downwind, since the force created by the sails is in any case in line with the direction of travel. In light wind, the centreboard is positively harmful, as it considerably increases the wetted surface area. It is thus better to retract it completely. In fresher winds, if your boat has no fixed underwater foil, it is worth keeping the centreboard down a little way. If there is no resistance to sideways movement, the boat becomes less controllable once it is anything other than dead downwind; the moment you head up, the boat begins to sideslip. What is more, there is no resistance to the boat rolling, so it loses directional stability.

The efficiency of the centreboard increases with the square of the speed through the water. If you are sailing fast, with little sideways pressure on the board, you do not need it very far down.

Clunk click...

rather than splash!

Strong winds

Downwind, things begin to liven up as the wind freshens. That gentle 'downhill' sail becomes a headlong rush, with rather poor brakes. The waves begin to take on more definite shape just as you begin to become aware of the amount of sail you are carrying and the speed at which you are travelling. You suddenly find the tiller demands much more attention...

At this stage, your first thought should be for the safety of boat and crew. It is hard to stop when you are sailing downwind, and if the spinnaker is up, every manoeuvre will take twice the time: returning to a member of the crew lost overboard can take a long while.

The first rule, which is valid for all points of sailing but especially vital downwind, is to clip yourself on in plenty of time, i.e. in anything but the lightest wind. The next rule is to know how long to keep the spinnaker hoisted. Different boats behave differently when the crew makes a mistake: a light dinghy will capsize without any breakage, though it might tip the crew in; a heavy cruiser will resist the capsize so hard that something might well break; and even a stable multihull can be flipped over in extremis.

The spinnaker can be kept up for a long while, so long as you have things under control. How long you leave it up depends largely on the skill and experience of the crew. You will only improve your spinnaker handling if you try it out in progressively stronger winds (making sure that any mishap will not have grave consequences, by sailing in suitably safe waters). We shall look shortly at the factors to take into account when deciding whether or not to carry the spinnaker.

The main problem when you are sailing downwind in heavy weather is staying on course. It is much easier to be slewed round by the sea or the wind than on any other point of sailing, and causes far more problems when it happens. It is seldom advisable to sail dead downwind: 10°–15° off will give you much improved stability and safeguard against broaches in either direction.

Helm balance
Instability caused by the sails

In a strong wind, the spinnaker can seriously upset the boat's directional stability. It becomes more difficult to keep the boat upright, and the spinnaker tends to heel the boat to windward, giving it lee helm.

Before you know it, the boat can start to roll, the tiller pulls in alternate directions and the helm starts to sweat…

It can also become more difficult to keep correct fore-and-aft trim, as the spinnaker can easily pull the top of the mast forward and lift

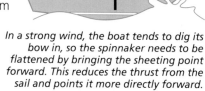

In a strong wind, the boat tends to dig its bow in, so the spinnaker needs to be flattened by bringing the sheeting point forward. This reduces the thrust from the sail and points it more directly forward.

the transom. The natural braking action of the water on the hull causes it to bury its bows. You can move aft to bring the bows up, but the best way of stabilising the boat is to flatten and steady the spinnaker by using a barber hauler or reaching hook to bring the tension on the clew down and forwards, then keeping the foot horizontal by doing the same for the tack.

If you will be subjecting the spinnaker to a long period of sustained tension, it is best to let the halyard up or down a few centimetres every couple of hours, just to prevent excessive wear at any one point.

Mainsail twist should be minimised by using kicking-strap tension; and the main should be trimmed so as to act counter to any rolling motion.

Instability caused by waves

The combination of waves and rolling brings a monohull off course. When a wave catches the boat on the windward quarter, it tends to make it luff up; and the boat will bear away when caught by a wave on the leeward quarter. The action of the wave can add to this pivoting effect by heeling the boat, increasing the tendency to go off course.

It is crucial to have a sensitive hand on the tiller in waves. Once the wave has caught the boat, the rudder has no effect, so you actually need to anticipate its action. If the swell is coming at your windward quarter, you need to bear away before the wave, so that it puts you back on course; if it is coming from the leeward quarter, you will need to luff before the wave and then let it push you back down to leeward with no fear of an accidental gybe.

All this requires firmness and skill on the tiller. In stormy seas, you maintain the harmony of boat and sea by adopting your best Wagnerian style, and conduct the pizzicato of the wavelets with suitably delicate strokes. In effect this means pushing or pulling the tiller only when there is most force from the wave trying to send it the other way: your aim is actually to keep the rudder as steady as possible. This simple task can often be physically quite exhausting.

One added complication: you need to learn different reflexes depending on the number of hulls your boat has!

Broaching

The boat can escape from the grasp of even the most attentive helm at times and luff up uncontrollably. Adding a spinnaker makes this situation even more delicate. Once the boat heels over on its ear and slows down with the wind on the beam, it has a nasty habit of staying that way, because the airflow over the spinnaker becomes reversed: it flows up from the foot and escapes around the sides as best it can. When this happens, be glad you reefed the main following the instructions which you can read in a few pages' time.

If you react to the luff sufficiently quickly while your boat still has enough way on, by pulling the tiller up to windward and letting go the spinnaker sheet, you can sometimes save the situation. If the boat has slowed down so much that it barely responds to the helm, it will simply stay there, with the spinnaker flogging and shaking all the spars. You need to get out of this position, and quick.

There is a simple, fast way out: let off the guy. The boat will come upright, the spinnaker deflate and you can easily pull it down.

If broaching is a worry for a monohull, it is fatal for a multihull. There can be no question of happily recovering from the broach, whichever way round it happens: it is always preferable to get the spinnaker tangled or gybe. Since you can never be entirely sure that the wind will not cause a sudden broach, the spinnaker guy should

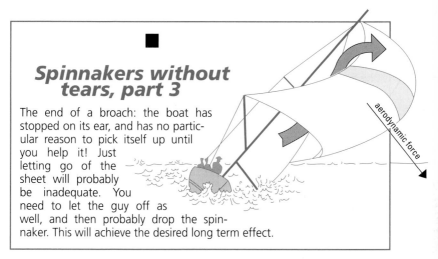

Spinnakers without tears, part 3

The end of a broach: the boat has stopped on its ear, and has no particular reason to pick itself up until you help it! Just letting go of the sheet will probably be inadequate. You need to let the guy off as well, and then probably drop the spinnaker. This will achieve the desired long term effect.

aerodynamic force

not be cleated, but should be held in the hand with two or three turns on a winch, ready for instant release if the situation demands.

Whatever boat you sail, never forget you have the option of dropping the spinnaker. This often improves the atmosphere considerably!

Accidental gybes
Monohulls
A broach can be embarrassing. Bearing off can be far worse, leading not only to an accidental gybe, but a broach on the opposite tack. If you have a boom preventer rigged, the resultant catastrophe can be truly spectacular, if short-lived: usually, something breaks rather quickly, and the spectacle is over.

When you are sailing downwind in waves, a boom preventer is nevertheless necessary. You need to ensure you are a safe 10°–15° away from dead downwind. All in all, the risk of a broach is infinitely preferable to the accidental gybe.

Multihulls
An accidental gybe following an uncontrolled bearing away is considerably less fearsome, and the chances of it happening are lower, since the boat rolls less. Since a broach can have horrible consequences, your reflex response to a problem should be to bear away, taking the chance of an accidental gybe. You should therefore be prepared for this eventuality.

You can prepare by:
- ■ eliminating mainsail twist;
- ■ cleating the mainsheet traveller in the middle of the boat or even to windward, so that the boom gybes automatically a long way over towards the shrouds without you needing to ease the mainsheet;
- ■ ensuring the mainsheet is always free to run out;
- ■ keeping everyone's head well below boom height;

45

■ not using a boom preventer, unless it is one which can free itself automatically.

There is a general principle hidden in all this, which cannot be repeated often enough: a multihull's safety depends on speed. You should do everything possible to prevent it slowing down, because once the rig is travelling faster than the hull...

Reducing sail

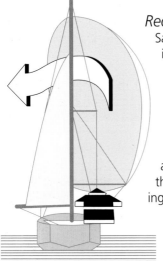

Sailing under spinnaker in a fresh breeze is not always easy. You must know when enough is enough, and cut your cloth according to your means.

Above a certain wind strength the problems caused by carrying the spinnaker start to outweigh the potential benefits. The spinnaker starts to cause an almost permanent roll which makes the boat difficult to steer. The risk of burying the bows increases drastically, even for a blunt-nosed boat; and if you do not break the mast, you might well end up sending the whole boat down.

Crew tiredness is a perfectly valid reason for taking the spinnaker down. You need to be alert and fit to tend a spinnaker in strong winds. It is also difficult to change places at the helm, because whoever has been steering while the wind was freshening will have been getting slowly used to the conditions, learning to react appropriately; any replacement, coming fresh to the job, is thrown in at the deep end, with no time to adjust to the situation before that wave or gust comes along which might cost you your spinnaker or your mast if incorrectly handled.

One more good reason for reducing sail in a strong wind. With a reef in the main, the air empties better from the spinnaker.

Running downwind under spinnaker in a big sea causes nervous exhaustion. Nobody on board can relax properly. Tiredness in turn can cause rash decisions to be taken. And this is before we have even raised the matter of losing someone overboard.

Knowing when you should not be carrying the spinnaker is thus vital if you are thinking of using one in strong winds. It is seldom any help to use a smaller spinnaker, as the problem is less one of area than of balance: as the spinnaker is only fixed at two points, it can subject the rigging to considerable strain. It is often much better to pole out the genoa or another jib, or to use an asymmetric spinnaker (which is by definition rigged without a pole). You may lose some speed, but you will make up for this by being able to hold your heading (as well as making your crew breathe more easily).

Light weather

In very light winds, it is just as exhausting running before the wind as in a strong breeze. In fact you can even find yourself longing for a few more of the problems which the excess of wind was giving you earlier. In light winds you can play with the spinnaker, which is not helping you along much, or you can amuse yourself by inventing go-faster tricks. The boat's rolling motion becomes your greatest enemy; and on a heavy boat (so long as you are not racing) you might just decide to drop all the sails for a while to give boat and crew a rest while you drift along.

It is worth knowing how to get your boat to move in the lightest of airs: this skill can be vital in a tricky passage as you need to make those few extra miles to avoid a foul tide, or simply to get back home on time.

Is it worth mentioning sail trim?

When you are running, the apparent wind is less strong than the true wind. As soon as the boat starts to move you feel no wind at all.

A light spinnaker (26gm per sq m) with light sheets (eg, 4mm diameter for a 100sq m sail) might just be persuaded to fill… but once you have got it filling, you have to keep it that way. You will almost certainly need to make constant adjustments to the tack height to keep it level with wherever the clew happens to be floating.

You might need to ease the halyard out slightly to keep the spinnaker well clear of the mainsail. This in turn has the disadvantage of decreasing the stability of the tack.

You can try to play the sails by letting them fill while gently easing the sheets, holding them once they reach the correct trim. You may have to hold them in place by hand if there is virtually no wind.

The sails must be as full as possible. If they flap a little as the boat rolls, all the better: the flapping can propel it forward.

The boat needs to be heeled slightly in order to get the sails filling in the right position. The crew should remain as still as possible. There is no point crouching down in the boat: you actually want all the windage you can get. If your boat has a centreboard, pull it up.

Whistling is said to encourage the wind to come…

To run or to reach?

Optimising course made good downwind

Modern boats, particularly multihulls, tend to be slow and uncomfortable on a run, so it is usual to avoid the run. Just as we were interested, when beating, to find the course which offered the most ground made good to windward, we seek the downwind course which makes most ground to leeward by exploiting the superior performance of our boat on a broad reach.

47

Reaching

The reach is that wide area between beating and running, which brings freedom and ease to the boat and its hard-pressed crew.

Reaching is the boat's natural and favoured condition. It travels fast and uses the wind efficiently. When the wind freshens on a beat, one's correct response is to ease the sheets; on the reach, you simply sheet in a bit more and travel all the faster. It is less a question of trimming them until the luff lifts than of working out the optimum angle through which they should deflect the airflow to give maximum power.

There is nevertheless one trap in store for the unwary. The rig can stall, slowing down suddenly and with no apparent reason. When this happens the wind seems to have disappeared completely and nothing you do has any effect.

Multihulls set one further trap for their crews: there is a greater risk of capsizing on the reach.

Points of reaching

There is a considerable difference in feel between sailing a boat with regular, laminar airflow over the sails, and the moment where the flow becomes turbulent. In the first case, we can speak of close or beam reaching, while the moment at which the flow becomes turbulent indicates that we are almost on a run: this is the area of the broad reach.

It is conventional, in fact, to divide the reach into close reaching and the rest. We shall begin by looking at the points of similarity between these two points of sailing, and then look at those areas which are unique to each. The differences in how you sail the boat on each point of sailing are as much a matter of personal preference and mood as of technical constraints. A reach can give you one of the most carefree rides in a boat or one of the most uncomfortable. It is perfectly possible to sail a reach without stalling, and even if you do stall, the effects need not be catastrophic; so long as you do not oversheet the sails, the boat will continue along quickly in any case. Nevertheless, there is always a risk with catamarans (especially the lighter types) that a mistake on the tiller will lead to a capsize, no matter how correctly you trim the sails.

If your aim is to extract maximum performance from your boat, you have to take the issue of stalling rather further. The greatest power is obtained from the sails when they are eased to the point of lifting (i.e. just when stalling is about to take place). At this point you need to stay on your guard.

Stalling

This is a matter we have dealt with several times. For the moment, we need to bear in mind simply that the sail creates gradually more power the closer it is sheeted, until it reaches a critical angle, at which it is said to stall, and the power falls away suddenly.

This critical angle is that at which the sail becomes an obstacle to the airflow rather than a deflector. The flow ceases to be regular and becomes turbulent, and the pressure of the wind on the sail suddenly drops.

When you have just stalled the sails, your first reaction is one of surprise. Nothing you noticed had prepared you for the stall, and you will take a moment or two to get over it. You need to free the sheets considerably or luff up a fair way to drive the turbulence off the sails before you can get back on course. If your boat is heavy, and the wind light, it can take a very long time to build your speed back up.

The apparent wind and its whims

One further important point to bear in mind is that the difference between the apparent wind and the true wind is greater on a reach than on any other point of sailing. The apparent wind comes from much further ahead than the true wind, and the difference increases the faster you go. (It can easily reach 30° on a dinghy and as much as 60°–80° on a multihull.) The smallest acceleration or deceleration can therefore mean a radical change in wind direction.

On a reach there can be considerable variation in the apparent wind.

Whenever the boat slows for any reason, the wind frees to such an extent that the sails are suddenly oversheeted; the airflow, which had been laminar, separates and becomes turbulent; the sails stall, and the initial slight deceleration can become a sudden stop if you maintain both sail trim and course as they were initially.

When bearing away from a close fetch, you can begin by increasing the fullness in the sails and thus the angle through which they deflect the wind. This gives maximum power as quickly as possible.

The further you bear away, the more the apparent wind angle reduces; this limits your ability to respond by easing the sheets, but it does mean that the boat accelerates to its critical speed more readily, as the increasing boat speed increases the relative wind, which in turn strengthens the apparent wind, giving yet more speed…

So long as the boat does not go beyond its critical speed, any fur-

49

ther bearing away will decrease the relative wind in proportion to the change in angle between the boat and the apparent wind. These two changes cancel each other out, so the boat can keep its speed, with the airflow over the sails remaining laminar, all the way round to about 140° from the true wind, so long as you do not stall the sails.

If the boat starts to plane, it will continue to accelerate as the angle between the boat and the apparent wind increases (even if the wind strength begins to drop). The most noticeable phenomenon in this case is that the apparent wind moves ahead only very slowly, and can stay below 50° even when the boat is sailing at 140° to the true wind (always assuming you have succeeded in keeping it on the plane). Once the boat's own speed becomes an important element in keeping the balance, you can imagine the concentration required on the part of the helm!

Boat speed

On a multihull the effect of slowing down is well known, and any crew will be wary of it. Basically, even a large boat can capsize simply as a result of slowing down suddenly. Let us spend some time looking at how this happens.

If we take the example of a catamaran which buries the leeward bow in a wave, the boat is suddenly slowed, the wind frees and the aerodynamic force on the sail suddenly increases and changes direction before the rig stalls. The boat develops weather helm and luffs, unless the helm has previously borne away in anticipation of the problem. If it is allowed to luff, the bow will be buried deeper, slowing the boat still more. Meanwhile the masthead continues forward at its usual merry pace and pow! the boat somersaults, throwing you all into the water.

This chain of events explains our earlier comment that the speed of a multihull is what ensures its safety. You must never allow a multihull to be slowed suddenly, especially on a reach.

The crew's instinct should be to maintain boat speed at all costs, even if this means bearing away a little. If you do need to slow the boat down, by all means luff up, but do so gradually and sparingly.

On a monohull you will in any case be travelling less fast. The boat can heel without any great danger, so feels quite different. Slowing down suddenly does have the same aerodynamic effects, but the boat can respond by heeling and losing power, so there are generally far fewer problems caused.

Sail trim

You should constantly be changing the angle at which you trim the sails, to correspond to the speed of the boat. The faster you travel, the further ahead the apparent wind comes, and the further in you need to sheet the sails to keep them at the optimum angle to the wind.

When the wind freshens, you do not need to flatten or twist the sails: it is enough simply to ease the sheets. This means that they deflect the wind less, but the force exerted on them by the wind will stay the same and will be pointed further forward, thus increasing the usable power at your disposal.

As always, the sails should be sheeted in until they just about stop lifting at the luff; they should not be oversheeted, which runs the risk of stalling them. You can spot a stall coming if you have tell-tales sewn into the sails; keeping a close eye on the tell-tales allows you to trim the sails perfectly, just to the limit of flow separation.

Spinnaker trim

The same principles apply here as when running.

To recap:

■ the pole should be at right angles to the apparent wind;
■ the spinnaker should be vertically symmetrical;
■ the pole should be at right angles to the mast;
■ the spinnaker needs to be flattened in strong winds.

These principles are subordinate only to the need to balance the boat, which might mean you have to change the angle of the pole to the apparent wind; occasionally the pole will also have to be at a different angle to the mast, in order to keep the foot horizontal.

On a reach, the spinnaker generally flattens itself naturally, since you are pulling the clew further down the closer to the wind you go and the further inboard you sheet the sail. In light winds, the sheet should be led further back and higher (up to the pulpit, or even the boom end) to keep the sail full; as the wind freshens, the sheet fairlead should go forward and down to flatten the sail.

You can also buy reaching spinnakers which are cut less full than running spinnakers and are designed to allow you to carry them closer to the wind. The tack of these spinnakers needs to set

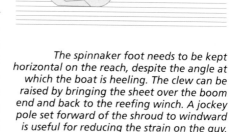

The spinnaker foot needs to be kept horizontal on the reach, despite the angle at which the boat is heeling. The clew can be raised by bringing the sheet over the boom end and back to the reefing winch. A jockey pole set forward of the shroud to windward is useful for reducing the strain on the guy.

fairly low: you can tell the correct height by checking the position of the fold on the luff of the spinnaker when you ease the sheet. Most spinnakers curl first at the shoulder, i.e. approximately two-thirds of the way up.

If the fold appears higher up, you have the tack too low; if the fold is lower, the pole is set too high.

Some reaching spinnakers are trimmed the opposite way round from downwind spinnakers. The tack height is adjusted first, using the luff fold to find the correct height; the clew is then trimmed to make the spinnaker vertically symmetric. Starcut spinnakers need the luff rather tighter than others, as they are used more like a genoa, and on these the fold should appear half-way up. Asymmetric spinnakers are intermediate sails between spinnakers and genoas, and these too should set with the foot horizontal.

Boat trim

Many monohulls tend to develop strong weather helm on a reach, since the centre of effort of the sails is so far down to leeward.

It is very difficult to counter this tendency. If you have a pivoting centreboard, you can raise it most of the way and offset most of the weather helm. The most important thing is to ensure that the boat stays flat, since the slightest heel increases the weather helm still further.

Close to beam reaching

A non-planing boat sails fastest on a close or beam reach. The airflow over the sails is regular, with the aerodynamic force strong and pointed well forward. In a fresh breeze, however, the boat can develop a considerable heeling couple, and you will need to lean well out to keep the sails trimmed at their optimum angle to the wind. It is hard work, but worth it!

The reach is a sort of half-way house between running and close-hauled. It gives you the greatest freedom of choice in how you trim the boat and sails. The sails can be sheeted anywhere between their stalling point and flapping. Even if they do stall, the recovery is quicker on a reach than otherwise: you simply let them go to get rid of the turbulence, then sheet back in gradually, picking up power and speed as you re-establish laminar flow.

In the gusts, you can choose whether to luff, as if you were on a beat, or to bear away and ease the sheets, depending on the conditions and where you are headed.

Spinnaker or genoa?

Deciding which foresail to use can be a tough problem. You cannot always tell in advance which will be more efficient. In the diagram, we show the borderline case where either one, along with appropriate mainsail trim, will give the same result.

In order to keep the spinnaker drawing, you have to sheet it in fairly hard, with the result that its power is not directed so far forward as you would like. The genoa gives less power, but it is directed further forward. Even so, the spinnaker has the advantage at this point. Under genoa, however, you can afford to ease the mainsail further, giving much better directed power than under spinnaker. The greater power of the combined spinnaker and mainsail has to be weighed against the better direction of the force provided by genoa and main together.

When you do decide to hoist the spinnaker, you can get a very approximate idea of the direction in which it is pulling, by looking at the halyard.

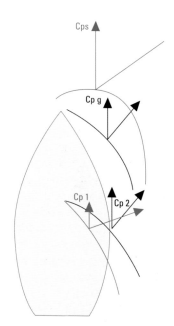

Cp1 + Cps = Cp2 + Cpg. In other words, the spinnaker and genoa are equally efficient.

The only time a spinnaker is really useful on a close reach is in light airs. When there is more wind, any speed gained has to be offset against the extra distance you will need to sail due to the inevitable broaches, plus the time needed for pulling the sail up and down.

Multihulls

Some multihulls start to plane even on a close reach. Since the apparent wind is then well ahead, the sails will be sheeted almost as tight as for a beat. The only difference should be that you increase the angle of deflection by allowing more camber in the sails.

The boat needs to be sailed differently on a close reach, because of the risk of a capsize. You must not allow the boat to broach or to stop suddenly, and you must be very careful not to allow it to bury a bow. At the slightest hint of a problem, you should react by bearing away. This is a difficult habit to pick up if you have spent years in a monohull before changing over to a multihull, but it must be acquired if you want to hang on to your new boat!

Beam to broad reaching

Beyond the beam reach, there should be no question about it: up with the spinnaker!

It has to be said that the boat is in the greatest danger of stalling on this point of sailing. As you bear away from a close reach, you ease the sails gradually to keep them correctly trimmed to the wind, until the moment comes when the main is against the shroud. At that stage, bearing away any further will result in stalling.

Even if you keep rigidly to that course, there is still a good chance of stalling at some stage, simply if a little wave slows you a touch. When this does happen, you cannot recover by easing the sails any further, so you need a good strong luff, almost such that the sails flap. Then you can start to bear away carefully back on to your course.

There is an enormous difference between sailing the reach with laminar airflow and sailing it with turbulent flow. It is quite possible to see two boats sailing the same broad reach, with the same sail trim, at markedly different speeds: one of them has borne away on to the reach, maintaining laminar flow, and is still sailing fast; the other has just luffed up from a run and is still dawdling along with turbulence on the downwind side of its sails. It can pick up speed by a short, hefty luff, but until it does, it might as well be in a different world from its faster neighbour.

There can be no question about the correct way to sail a broadish reach in a more-or-less constant wind. When a gust hits, you have nothing to gain by luffing up: that will simply overpower the boat. You should always bear away and ease the sheets, in monohulls or in multihulls. If the gust is really strong, bearing away sharply can take the sting out of it by stalling the sails. As the flow becomes turbulent, it exerts less force on the sails. You can use the stall as an important safety valve on multihulls when absolutely necessary.

2

CHANGING TACK

Changing tack is a peculiar moment on board a boat, and an activity unlike any other: very briefly, the boat actually pushes either its bow or its stern through the eye of the wind. The sails, which are normally trimmed in or out fairly gradually, are subjected to sudden movements from one side of the boat to the other. In all this motion, there is a momentary hiatus, an instant of uncertainty, which you must learn to control.

The eye of the wind is like a wall: you can luff up close to it, travelling forward as you do so, but to get over the wall, you need to use all the momentum you have been able to build up. Just as when you are beating, keeping way on is of paramount importance when you tack.

Gybing can be done without much concern for boat speed. It is more important when you gybe to ensure that you have your course under control, as any deviation from the plan can foul everything up. When you are running before the wind, it is a little like balancing as you walk along the top of the wall, and the gybe must not be allowed to knock you off!

There is thus a world of difference between the two ways of changing tack.

Tacking

Tacking is a decisive sort of manoeuvre. The boat heads up into the wind beyond its close-hauled course, continues luffing right through the eye of the wind, and you end up close-hauled on the opposite tack. Nothing simpler!

However, as this manoeuvre is taking place, the sails flap, and the boat is supposed to travel through an angle of 90° powered by nothing more than its own momentum; if there is insufficient momentum or it is used incorrectly, the boat might fail to make it all the way through the eye of the wind, and you can be caught *in irons*, that is, stuck temporarily head to wind. This is usually no more than embarrassing, though it can on occasion be dangerous.

We do not want to exaggerate the chances of a tack turning dangerous, but we do insist that a tack must not be allowed to fail. Even if we appear a little paranoid on the subject, please do us the favour of taking this point very seriously. A failed tack in a fresh breeze, just off a lee shore, has to be one of the most common causes of serious yachting accidents. And failing to tack means that you have failed to come to terms with the way the boat interacts with the sea and wind around it.

There are numerous conditions which must be fulfilled in order for a tack to succeed. The main ones are:

■ the boat must be correctly balanced, and neither under- nor over-canvassed;

■ the helm must take account of the state of the waves, and choose the right moment to make the move;

■ the manoeuvre must be started from a close-hauled course, with way on;

■ both tiller and sheets must be correctly handled throughout, and the boat's trim needs appropriate adjustment.

When the weather is kind, it is possible to tack successfully while observing only two or three of these conditions. The moment the wind or the sea gets up, however, you can ill afford any failure, and then you must get everything right.

We shall go into some detail now, looking at the procedure for tacking a cruising yacht in a strong breeze, which should demonstrate the principles and pitfalls involved.

Preparations

Starting from close-hauled

There is a bit of a sea running, a strong wind, we are getting close to the shore (for example) and it is almost time to tack.

The first step is to make sure the boat is sailing a close-hauled course. If you try to tack starting from any other point of sailing, the boat has too great an angle to travel through without propulsion: then there is a risk that you will run out of steam before the boat even reaches head to wind.

For this reason, at least at the beginning, you should be sailing close-hauled for a little while before you start to tack, just long enough to make sure you really know where the wind is coming from, the boat is well set up and travelling fast enough to make it round.

■ The boat really is close-hauled. (We defined this as being the course which makes the maximum ground to windward.)

On multihulls, this definition can often mean sailing a freer course which leaves a considerable dead angle. It may then be worth while adopting a rather closer course than that you would normally expect to sail, even at some cost to your boat speed.

■ The boat is 'well set up'. We take this as meaning that the sails are correctly trimmed, just short of lifting; the windward runner (or backstay) is tightening the forestay; all crew members are well back from the bow so they do not slow its turn through the wind and waves or get in the way of the airflow in the slot between jib and

58

main; the boat is correctly canvassed, so it has enough power but not so much it is hard to control. Basically, the helm should feel good.

You can tell that a monohull is correctly set for the tack by checking that it is not heeling excessively. This check is meaningless on a multihull, so you need to spend a little more time feeling your way into the boat's movements to gauge whether it is ready.

■ The boat is travelling fast enough: the lighter the boat and the less momentum it has, the more important speed becomes as you go into the tack. This is especially true with catamarans.

Make sure all the conditions for a successful tack have been fulfilled, i.e. that when you choose to tack, you will be able to do so.

All the above conditions are really nothing more than you would expect of a boat sailing a good close-hauled course. Don't strangle the boat's natural rhythm to set it up for the tack. If you like, the boat does not need to know you are getting ready to go about.

Try to choose your moment to tack, so there is no chance of the sea itself destroying your hard-won momentum or turning you off course. This means avoiding any waves which look particularly large or powerful; particularly on a multihull, which will end up going through the same wave two or even three times as it tacks. You need to be able to delay the tack if the boat is suddenly slowed for any reason, since speed is the most important condition for getting started.

Successful tacking also results from perfect co-ordination among the crew: everyone has their own job to perform at a precise moment. To co-ordinate all the separate activities, the skipper can give direct orders loudly as the tack takes place. Some picturesque cries from the age of the square-rigger have been lost as tacking becomes less dramatic, but there is still a fairly well established sequence of orders: 'Ready about!' is first, at which the crew confirm they are indeed ready, then 'Lee-oh!' and, soon after, the order to let the sheets fly. We shall use this sequence to look at the whole procedure in some detail, as each order corresponds to a precise set of actions. Of course, you

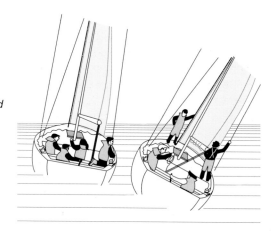

The left-hand boat is ready to go about:
■ *it is close-hauled;*
■ *the sails are well trimmed;*
■ *the forestay is tight;*
■ *it is correctly canvassed for the wind;*
■ *it is heeling only slightly;*
■ *the crew members are in position;*
■ *the sheets are free. If only we could say the same for the right-hand boat!*

can try your own variations. There are even skippers who prefer four-letter words to browbeat their reluctant crew.

'Ready about!'

This serves as a general alert. Everyone heads for a predetermined position. You check that all the sheets are free to run.

■ The windward jib sheet should have some slack in it, and be lying free on the foredeck, so the jib pulls it across the deck clear of the numerous obstacles. It is pointless, and can be positively harmful, to take a pre-emptive turn on the winch before tacking: this just means extra work for whoever is looking after the winch handle. Check this is in place, in easy reach.

■ The leeward sheets should be ready for release, and free to run easily. To ensure a sheet is free, leave it flaked in an orderly snaking pile on the cockpit floor, don't coil it. It might be worth while to let off one or two turns on the winch to let the jib out more quickly later. Beware, though: the best thing at this stage is not to release anything.

■ If the leeward runner can be tightened before tacking without ruining the shape of the mainsail, now is the time to do so. Otherwise, this must be done as you begin the tack, just as the mainsail starts to flap. The other runner is eased only after the tack.

■ When the crew is ready, they confirm 'jib ready' or 'staysail ready'. The helm also should confirm their readiness, if they are not the skipper. If a mealtime is coming up, check there will be no massive upset in the galley as the angle of heel changes.

Choose exactly the right moment, with the boat in tune with the rhythm of the swell and not at the start of a series of huge waves: there is nothing so destructive to a boat's momentum as a massive wave pushing it back on to the original tack a third of the way through, particularly multihulls. If the waves are steep, begin the turn high on the back of a wave, just after the crest, so you are in the trough as the bow passes through the wind. The next wave then gives impetus to the move off on the new tack.

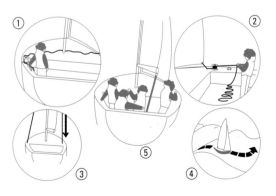

1 There is slack in the windward jib sheet.
2 The leeward sheet is flaked on the cockpit floor.
3 The leeward runner is tightened.
4 The big wave is safely out of the way.
5 Time to go about.

'Lee-oh!'

This is the point of no return, the order to charge. It commits you, your boat, your crew, even the sea itself, to a course of action. When you say 'Lee-oh!', the boat has to make its turn, and every available means has to be used to this end. Let us look at who does what.

What does the helm do?

Any sudden tiller movement can stop the boat in its tracks: the rudder acts as a brake, and the boat is halted by any attempt to turn too tightly.

On the other hand, handling the tiller too timidly means that the boat luffs up too slowly, losing momentum all the way.

Theoretically, then, what the helm needs to do is to push the tiller gently at first, then increase the angle as the boat turns, accompanying the tack with the tiller movements. Often, however, the boat can tack just as well or even better if left to its own devices. The helm can actually push the tiller away, then leave it and turn to looking after the mainsheet. Whether or not you need to keep hold of the tiller, you can help the tack by pulling down on the mainsheet above the bottom block without letting it out of the cleat. This has the effect of making the boat luff: the sail is used like a rudder in the air. The momentary oversheeting and the masthead inertia also increase the heel in a monohull, thus making the boat luff still more quickly.

What does the crew do?

If necessary, one crew member can help trim the mainsail, or take this task over entirely. One tightens the jib, by pulling sideways on the sheet between winch and fairlead (with the sheet still cleated, of course).

As you luff up, the other crew mem-

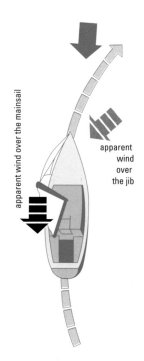

apparent wind over the mainsail

apparent wind over the jib

As the boat rotates, the apparent wind frees the jib and backs the main.

'Strength means knowing the right way to tackle the job.' – Turkish proverb.

61

bers should move forward and to leeward, to accentuate the heel and make the boat luff faster. If the boat still will not tack after you have gone through all this, there is only one thing for it: get a new boat.

'Check the sheets!'

This order is directed at the foredeck, or jib, hand only. For the first time, the jib sheet is brought in to play properly.

Do not release the jib too quickly

It is important to have the jib as tight as possible as the tack begins, since it should be drawing as long as possible as you luff up; and it will keep drawing for longer than you think. The rotation of the boat causes a particular effect, so that the jib is actually freed by the apparent wind as the boat turns, and the mainsail is headed. The main starts to flap early on (at which stage the mainsheet can be eased), but the jib will continue to fill until you are almost head to (true) wind, using the apparent wind caused by the turn.

This extra little bit of thrust can be precious indeed, quite apart from stopping the jib flapping, which would in itself slow you down severely. The jib should be released only once it has lifted. This is the moment to wait for before giving the order to check sheets.

Do not pull it in too quickly

One crew member lets the old leeward jib sheet off quickly, if necessary pulling it forward of the fairlead. The jib will flap as it passes through the eye of the wind, so long as the new sheet is not pulled tight instantly. This ensures that the sheet pulls clear automatically of any obstacles on the foredeck. The boat keeps turning under its own momentum at this stage. It gets through the eye of the wind and starts to bear away. The mainsail fills of its own accord on the new tack and the helm begins to stop the turn by re-centring the tiller.

Have you made it? Well, yes, assuming that the new sheet was not pulled tight before the boat was well past head-to-wind. The classic mistake of novice crews, and the commonest cause of a failed tack, is wanting to sheet the jib in before it is ready, and the very moment its clew has got past the mast. All that happens is that the jib fills from the wrong side, stops the boat dead, and starts to turn it back in the opposite direction. The mistake lies in not realising that the fairlead is some distance from the middle of the boat. It is not enough for the boat to be past head-to-wind: the line from the tack to the fairlead has to be through the axis of the wind as well, so that the jib is flapping almost next to the shroud before it is sheeted tight.

To spot the correct moment, you have to keep a careful eye on the jib's movement. Many novice crews, at this stage, start to con-

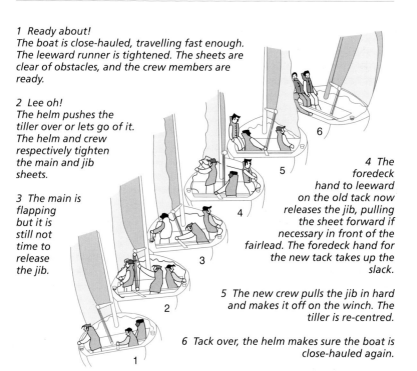

1 Ready about!
The boat is close-hauled, travelling fast enough. The leeward runner is tightened. The sheets are clear of obstacles, and the crew members are ready.

2 Lee oh!
The helm pushes the tiller over or lets go of it. The helm and crew respectively tighten the main and jib sheets.

3 The main is flapping but it is still not time to release the jib.

4 The foredeck hand to leeward on the old tack now releases the jib, pulling the sheet forward if necessary in front of the fairlead. The foredeck hand for the new tack takes up the slack.

5 The new crew pulls the jib in hard and makes it off on the winch. The tiller is re-centred.

6 Tack over, the helm makes sure the boat is close-hauled again.

centrate on the movement of their own hands pulling on the sheet; but the time to start admiring one's handiwork is after the job is done, not during the manoeuvre. It is generally the case that one should carry out common manoeuvres without looking at one's own hands. However, in the case of tacking this general rule becomes the first condition of success.

Do not pull it in too slowly

When the jib has made it all the way across the boat, and it is time to sheet it in, do not waste any time about it! Once the jib fills with wind, it can become very difficult to control: ideally, you want to sheet it tight just at the instant where it cannot quite fill. After only a little practice, it becomes quite easy to spot this precise instant. If you miss it, and have to pull the jib in while it is already filling, you will need strong arms and a good winch! If you have no winch, you might even find it necessary to bear away so that the airflow becomes turbulent and there is less power in the jib. This might be a fairly crude solution to the problem, but it is certainly better than luffing up and slowing the boat down badly.

Overlapping jibs

There are special difficulties associated with tacking with an overlapping jib (and some boats can sail with their biggest jib up even in

63

quite fresh weather). As the jib foot extends well aft of the mast, it is sometimes hard for the clew to make it round the front of the mast as you carry out the tack. If the clew does not get caught on a shroud, it catches on a halyard or some eye on the front of the mast. You quite often need someone to give it an extra hand round.

The most efficient procedure is for the person who releases the old sheet to hold on to the clew and walk it all the way to the mast, keeping hold throughout. On a fresh day, this job should be entrusted to your best heavyweight crew member. Even so, a moment's inattention can leave the heavyweight looking like an amateur boxer after going ten rounds with a professional.

On a large yacht, having a crew member perched in the bow will make little difference to the boat's fore-and-aft trim. This allows you to rig a webbing tacking-line, sewn to the jib at the centre of the foot, with one arm either side of the forestay. The crew pulls the foot forward sufficiently for the clew to make it round the mast. This frees the jib hand in the cockpit to help get the jib sheeted in on the new tack: firstly, by helping pull the old jib sheet forward, then by pulling down on the clew until the jib is properly sheeted in and cleated.

Twin headsails

If your boat has twin headsails, you need to sheet in the jib first, then the staysail. One crew member can handle the pair of them in succession. If you do it the other way round, the jib clew flaps furiously against the back of the tight staysail, and both sails can wear out very quickly. What is more, sheeting the jib in actually makes it easier to sheet the staysail. The opposite does not work.

To conclude

Whatever else happens, one thing should now be clear: that no crew member should be sitting idle while the boat tacks. The success of the whole manoeuvre depends largely on the co-ordinated activity of all on board: the tack can be ruined by an attack of excess zeal; or it can be just as seriously hindered by a laid-back attitude along the lines of 'What's the point in pulling the sheet in when we're just about to let it off again?'.

The stronger the wind, the more important it becomes to prepare for the tack calmly and spend time getting every condition right for success. It is far better to take your time and be certain you will make it (even if that means you sail very close to some obstacle while making sure you have enough boat speed), than to throw your boat around in a series of hasty and ill-executed attempts at a tack.

Who does what: the well organised tack

Helm (H)	Foredeck hand (F)	Mainsail hand (M)	Skipper (S)
1 Steers close-hauled			Chooses the moment. Checks: Ready about?
2	Goes to leeward	Centres mainsheet traveller then stays ready, sheet in hand	Checks the crew has understood and is in position, ready
3 Replies: ready!	Ready!	Ready!	Gives the order: Lee oh!'
4 Luffs gradually	Uncleats jib	Trims mainsail in	
5 Luffs harder	Waits for jib to flap, then frees fast		
6 Allows boat to turn at its own speed, accompanying the turn until close fetching on new tack	Moves quickly to the new side and sheets in	Frees slightly	
7 Gently centres tiller	Trims jib using winch		
8 Picks up close-hauled course	Fine-trims jib	Trims main and positions traveller according to wind strength	

Making sure of the tack

When you have reason to suspect a tack might go awry, there is one technique you can use to ensure success.

You can actually tack without touching the jib. Once you have made it through the eye of the wind, the jib fills from the other side and pushes the boat round. It is then released and sheeted in only after the tack is complete. Doing it this way, you will certainly not come out of the tack with much speed on, and you will have to bear away considerably to pick up speed again.

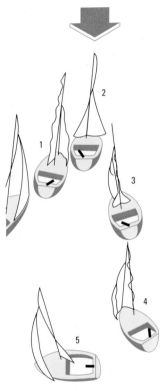

If you find yourself head to wind with the sails flapping, either because of a wrong move, or because you had insufficient way on to make the tack, you can still get round if you react swiftly.

If, for example, you are caught in irons while you are trying to tack to port:

■ hold the jib sheet out against the wind, with the sail backed, on the starboard side of the boat;

■ push the boom out to port, leaning down on it to limit the twist;

■ reverse the tiller (i.e. push it over to port), as the water will flow over the back face of the rudder as the boat sails backward.

The combined effect of the two sails and the rudder will push the boat round so it comes out on the port tack.

Once the boat is well on its way on the port tack, you can let go the boom, release the jib, pick up some speed on a beam reach and then come back on to a close-hauled course, sheeting the sails in progressively as you go.

On a catamaran, you need to release the sails the moment the boat starts to move backwards; otherwise the boat picks up too much speed as it travels backwards, and puts excessive strain on the rudders and fittings.

Caught in irons...
1 The boat runs out of steam, head to wind.
2 Jib and mainsail are held out deliberately backed, with the tiller reversed.
3 Jib and tiller are still reversed.
4 The boat bears away hard on to the new tack, and the jib is then released. The tiller returns to its usual position.
5 You pick up speed on the reach before beginning to luff back up on to the close-hauled course.

If you do not respond sufficiently quickly with this manoeuvre, the boat will fall back into irons and you have no choice but to start again from the beginning. This means picking up some speed on a reach before doing anything, so you can ease the sheets and wait for the boat to come round on to the reach of its own accord. Alternatively, you can speed up the manoeuvre by going through the same routine as above, but in the opposite direction: the jib then needs to be backed to port with the boom pushed out to starboard, and the tiller down to starboard. This will give you a quicker restart.

If you absolutely cannot afford for the tack to fail, you can always give a push round with the paddle: this can give you just that little bit of extra force which makes all the difference and saves the tack. It might even save the boat…

If things are really that difficult, it is tempting to use the motor to ensure that the tack succeeds. If you do take this step, remember that there must not be any sheets trailing in the water, and that the motor should not be run for extended periods while the boat is heeling. In other words, the motor should be on only briefly, and this might have the effect of running down the battery, since you cannot run it for long enough to recharge after using the current for the starter. Using the motor should therefore be an exception.

Handling characteristics

Not all boats handle similarly when they tack. The weight of the boat is more important than its size in this respect, as in many others. A light boat lacks momentum but can turn quickly; a heavier boat will keep its way on but turn slowly, no matter how small it is; and a multihull is light but turns slowly.

Some boats will tack more easily than others of the same weight, since factors such as hull shape and tuning also have an effect. In general, it is true to say that multihulls and boats of older designs are less willing to tack, whereas modern monohulls are much more obedient. Either way, you must get to know the reactions of your boat and not try to impose any unnatural rhythm on to your tacks.

As we conclude this section, what exceptions have we discovered to the rules covered at the beginning? We have spent this section describing techniques appropriate for relatively inexperienced crews and difficult weather conditions. In good weather, with a slick crew, a tack can be carried out flawlessly in less time than it takes to describe it. For instance, it is perfectly possible to tack from a point of sailing other than close-hauled if you can accompany the tiller movement with progressive changes to the sail trim. Just because your jib is allowed to flap too early does not necessarily mean your tack will fail, so long as the boat is travelling fast enough; and you can even carry the tack off with very little boat speed so long as you co-ordinate the tiller and sail movements perfectly.

This is no reason to get casual about tacking. One of the main perils with a monohull is that precisely because the boat does so much of the work itself, you tend to let the tack happen without paying much attention. After a while, you actually forget how the tack works and you fail at precisely the time you can least afford to: in bad weather, when you have not left yourself enough of a safety margin to recover in case of failure.

If this does happen to you, do not lose hope. You might not be able to tack round, but you may well be able to gybe.

Gybing

Gybing involves changing tacks with the wind behind you, but it does not necessarily mean changing direction. The mainsail will be completely eased for the run, and it rotates through almost 180° as it crosses the boat; the spinnaker also needs to change over to the new windward side, and the spinnaker pole needs to be moved on a monohull.

Gybing is probably the most delicate operation in all sailing as soon as there is more than a little wind. This is due in the first instance to the impossibility of 'turning the sails off'. When you tack, the mainsail flaps and loses all its power as you go through the manoeuvre; when you gybe, the mainsail is always drawing, even if you sheet it all the way in. (In fact, when that happens, the leech becomes the leading edge. Since it is not rigid, the leech flops from one side to the other, but the sail stays full either way.) The spinnaker never stops pulling; and in fact it goes through a phase in the gybe where it is pulling but not stabilised by the pole, so it really can develop a mind of its own!

The main problem in gybing is the risk of yawing. Although any downwind sailing carries this risk, the change in the boat's balance which occurs as the sails change sides aggravates it. Downwind, as we noted earlier, the boat is balancing along the top of a wall, and the available space between falling off either side is not great. Unfortunately, the boat devotes most of its time to trying to fall off! The helm needs to remain highly vigilant: otherwise the boat heads off on a wild broach to windward, or it ends up sailing by the lee and you find yourself gybing accidentally, the boom sweeping across the deck, destroying everything in its path, knocking the boat into a broach on the new tack and tying the spinnaker (sensitive soul that it is) in knots around itself. This sort of gybe usually ends up breaking something.

Who does what: the gybe

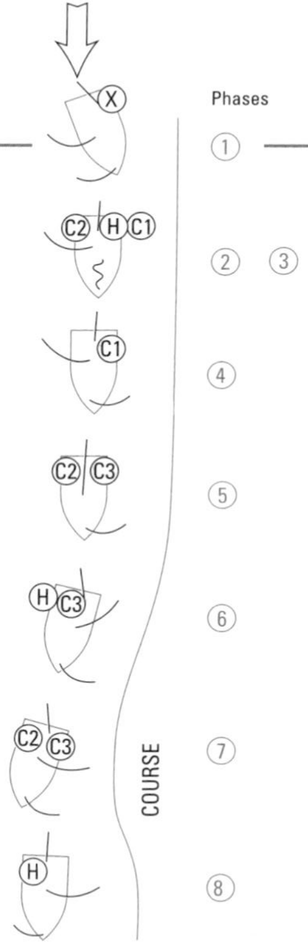

Helm (H)	Crew 1	Crew 2	Crew 3
1 Gets ready	Gets ready	Gets ready	Gets ready
2 Holds downwind course		Brings mainsheet traveller to centre	
3	Releases leeward jib sheet		
4	Brings jib across to goosewinged		
5 Holds downwind course	Trims jib to keep it drawing	Sheets main to centre	Tightens leeward backstay
6 Bears away a few degrees			Frees off leeward backstay
7		Lets out mainsheet as required. Frees leeward traveller	Adjusts new windward backstay
8 Bears away on to downwind course	If necessary, helps the jib over to goosewinged		

Phases

COURSE

There are certain precise conditions under which you can be sure a gybe will not end in this sort of disaster:

■ *The boat should be sailing dead downwind*, and retain exactly the same heading throughout the manoeuvre.

■ *Monohulls should be kept dead flat* throughout. The worst enemy is the rhythmical downwind roll known as the 'death roll'. This leaves you one-legged on top of your wall!

■ Even more than usual, *sheets and controls must be kept clear*. In particular, the mainsheet, which might need to run free at any time, must be ready for an immediate release.

■ Last but not least, do not hurry! Unlike a tack, the gybe does not suffer from being done at a snail's pace, and boat speed is unimportant. The manoeuvre itself does not necessarily mean that the boat is actually changing course, and you have some flexibility over the time you elect to take over it. All the same, whether you work out your gybe routine in minute detail or not, there should be one person on board co-ordinating the work, as the individual crew members are working fairly spread out, and someone is needed to retain an overall view of what is going on at any one time.

Just as for the tack, we shall now go through the essentials of gybing a one-, two- or three-hulled vessel in a fresh wind and moderately rough sea, since only in this case will really interesting problems crop up.

Preparations

Bearing away to a dead run

Steering on a run is never easy: it is difficult to feel where the wind is; your tell-tales do not give a clear picture; and the boat barely changes its angle of heel as you alter course. Nevertheless, before gybing, you need to be sailing dead downwind. How can you go about achieving this?

The spinnaker can give you the best rough guide. Assuming it is correctly trimmed, it will have the pole guyed square across the wind and the clew not far from the forestay. If there is a fold to be seen on the luff, this shows that you are a good 15° above the dead run. If, instead, the spinnaker is a little floppy and seems to be in danger of collapsing, you are already sailing by the lee. In fact, this guide is at best rough: a real dead run is much more precise than this, and spotting it is largely a matter of practice: the helm's ears can sense the wind, just as the burgee can; and the direction of the waves and behaviour of the boat can give a good idea too.

You decide to gybe. Your mental check-list should ensure you do not forget any of those little things which cause great upsets:

■ have you eased both backstays? This should have been done as soon as you bore away below a beam reach;

■ is the kicking strap tight? Doing this limits mainsail twist, thus also limits the boat's tendency to roll; it also ensures you do not make the famous boom-in-the-air 'Chinese gybe';

■ is the mainsheet traveller cleated centrally? This should be done in case you need to be able to sheet the main in centrally as you gybe; and in any case, it is a simple matter of looking after your equipment to ensure that the traveller cannot shoot all the way across the boat at top speed following the sail;

■ have you let off the boom preventer? Forgetting to do this is a more frequent cause of upsets than you would believe…

As all this checking is going on, the helm must also keep an eye on the boat's course to ensure that it stays on the dead run. Nothing must be allowed to obstruct your view of what is going on (including affectionate spouses, children or others sitting on your knee). Many people prefer to helm through the gybe while standing – though making allowance for the boom coming across – as this gives a good feel for the balance of the boat and can help you respond more quickly to the movements of the mainsail and the spinnaker.

At the same time, in a monohull, in waves, you have to be careful not to allow the 'death roll' to get started. A good way of stopping a death roll is to give the tiller a good hard shake to left and right. (Trying to steer against the roll directly seldom works, and often makes it worse.) We do not know exactly why this works, but it does seem to.

Now you can carry out your gybe. Every crew member should have a clearly defined job, and there are plenty of jobs to be done: both spinnaker sheets need to be handled, as does the mainsheet; and you probably want someone on the foredeck to look after the spinnaker pole if there is space.

There are three phases to the operation:
■ moving the pole from one side to the other;
■ passing the mainsail across;
■ passing the spinnaker across.

1 Position the boat on a dead run.
2 Pass the pole across.
3 Sails change sides.
4 Final adjustments.

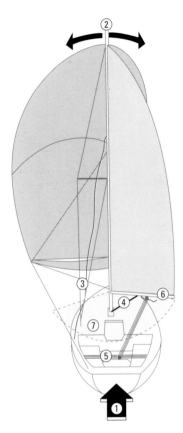

The helm's mental check-list:
1 Are we really on a dead run?
2 Has the boat stopped rolling?
3 Are the runners eased?
4 Is the kicking strap tight?
5 Is the traveller at the middle of the horse?
6 Did we remember to take the boom preventer off?
7 Is anyone standing in the way of the boom?

The final two phases have to occur at about the same time and they effectively constitute the gybe itself.

Moving the pole

The first thing to do is to make some space on the foredeck, so take down any big boy, reacher or spinnaker staysail you might have rigged; you also ease off the pole downhaul.

There are a number of different techniques for transferring the spinnaker pole from one side to the other. Whichever method you use, it will work only if the spinnaker will hold itself up and stay full without the pole, so long as the boat is held on its course dead downwind throughout the manoeuvre. In fact, when you are on a dead run, the spinnaker pole's function is less to hold the tack out from the mast than to keep the sail in. (This is because the sail has a natural tendency, on a run, to come round to windward.) This should mean that you can completely unrig the pole if you want, without needing to hurry to rig it back up.

How you move the pole across depends primarily on the rig of the boat.

If there is no inner forestay, or the inner forestay is removable, the pole can be swivelled round on its mast fixing in a circle, passing between the forestay and the mast. This is a simple procedure: you unclip the guy from the outer end of the pole, turn the pole round and clip it on to the sheet. (Occasionally, you will have to ease the sheet a little in order to be able to catch it; if your boat is rigged with double sheets, you need to catch the slack one.) If the inner forestay is fixed, the job becomes a little more complex. The pole is unclipped from the mast, pushed forward so that its inner end passes in front of the inner forestay, then brought back on the new side to bring the outer end past the forestay.

A twin-pole system can simplify matters considerably. As you start the gybe, the second pole is clipped to the leeward side of the mast and also to the sheet. (If you have double sheets, the pole can be rigged well in advance and attached to the slack sheet.) After the mainsail has been gybed, the new spinnaker guy is trimmed for the new tack and the first pole, which is now no longer in use, is removed.

One important detail should not be missed: the moment a spinnaker pole is unclipped from the guy, the uphaul must also be eased. If this is not done, the pole will stick up in the air by the spinnaker, with a chance of making a hole in the sail.

Whichever method you use, moving the spinnaker pole can become a tricky and often acrobatic job in a fresh wind and a swell. In these conditions you can see how huge are the forces acting on the spinnaker; trying to work against these forces is fruitless and exhausting. It is far better to use some cunning and ensure the forces are working with you, by watching the spinnaker's movements, waiting and then making your move at the instant where the force is pushing the sail where you want it to go. Once the sail is detached from the pole, it is free to move (and does, in the most disconcerting way). There can be no hard and fast rules about how to deal with this: the helm holds the key to the problem, by controlling the boat's course, so it is up to the helm to control the spinnaker for this difficult period.

If you cannot manage the situation perfectly, you should not feel obliged to gybe the spinnaker by putting the pole up with the sail still flying. It is perfectly possible to drop the spinnaker, gybe the main, put the pole up on the new tack and then hoist the spinnaker once more…

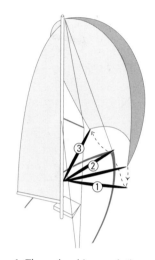

1 The uphaul is eased, then the pole unclipped.
2 The pole is passed under the forestay.
3 The pole is clipped back on to the sheet.

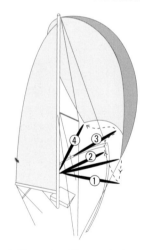

1 The uphaul is eased, then the pole unclipped.
2 The outer pole end is rested at the bottom of the forestay.
3 The pole is unclipped from the mast and the inner end passed forward of the inner forestay. The outer end is passed inside the forestay.
4 The inner end is clipped to the mast and the outer end finally clipped on to the sheet.

73

Gybing the sails

Once the spinnaker pole is in place, to leeward, you can begin the gybe proper, which consists in passing both sails, the spinnaker and the mainsail, to the other side of the boat, ideally at the same time.

Gybing the mainsail

Normal method

In light weather, you can gybe the mainsail without sheeting it in, by taking all the mainsheet strands in one hand, above the block, and swinging the sail into the centre of the boat and over to the other side.

One word of advice: *duck!*

This method of gybing is very common in dinghies, but is only of limited use in a cruiser. You must not underestimate the strength of the wind in the sail: it can be very hard work to get the boom into the middle, and nigh on impossible to stop it slamming over on to the new tack. If this happens, the boom itself can damage people or equipment, but so can the mainsheet, which has been known to catch unwary crew members in one or other of its loops and throw them bodily overboard.

This quick method is not suited to all rigs. It should not be used above force 2 with gaff- or gunter-rigged boats. With a bermudan rig you can use this method in fresher winds, so long as your boat has an effective kicking strap. (Without a good kicking strap, it could end in a Chinese gybe.)

On a monohull without a great deal of inbuilt stability, this method can become risky: it has a habit of ending in an enormous broach, with the crew falling overboard.

It should not be used in strong winds in any boat, because the mainsail transfers stress too suddenly to the rigging, with a substantial risk of breakage.

It is also possible to gybe the mainsail by pulling the kicking strap across. This is more easily done under spinnaker than under jib.

Traditional method

The traditional method of gybing is a better bet in fresh winds. Keeping the boat sailing straight downwind and well balanced, you begin to sheet in the mainsail. This gives the boat a tendency to luff up, and you will need to offset this by pulling the tiller. Once the sail is entirely sheeted in, you need only a slight change in direction, and the mainsail will fill from the new side; you can then free the mainsheet quickly, and again compensate for the boat's tendency to luff up on the new tack. To avoid the possibility of a broach, the sheet has to run all the way out to the figure-of-eight knot (which stops it in the bottom block before the boom hits the shroud).

... and gybing the spinnaker

Ideally, the spinnaker is gybed across at the same time as the mainsail, so that the two sails swap sides. This is the most sensitive moment in the manoeuvre. The mainsail must not be allowed to blanket the spinnaker at any stage, or the spinnaker will simply collapse around the forestay as it is starved of air. Similarly, the spinnaker needs to be transferred from one side of the boat to the other in a smooth movement: if you sheet in the new guy without letting off the sheet, the sail will stall and collapse; and if you let the sheet off without pulling the guy in sufficiently quickly, it will flap. (Flapping is preferable to collapsing.) It is therefore essential to co-ordinate the crew members who are looking after the spinnaker sheets. They should be given the opportunity to practise. A well synchronised gybe can be an incredibly satisfying achievement.

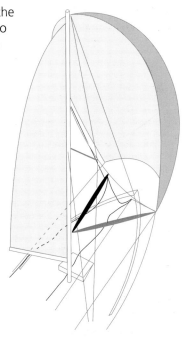

This boat has a complete set of sheets and pole for both tacks. The guy for the next tack can be put in place well before the gybe. It is attached to the clew, run through its own pole end and back down to the block on the deck. When you gybe, you simply need to tighten the guy and adjust the pole height. The sheet which is currently not in use stays in position and will only come under tension when the guy is eased, before the pole is lowered down to have its outer end placed on the deck. In the diagram, the boat has just gybed, and the only job remaining is to lower the outer end of the port pole to deck level.

Errors and handling characteristics

Classic mistakes

Luffing before the gybe. If the boat is not on a dead run when you start to sheet in for the gybe, the boat will tend to luff up strongly and becomes difficult to steer.

Accidental gybe. If the boat starts sailing by the lee without your noticing it, the mainsail can crash across the boat quite unexpectedly. This sort of gybe is always violent, and often ends in a capsize or some sort of breakage.

■ Who does what: gybing the spinnaker

Helm (H)	Crew 1	Crew 2	Crew 3
1 Gets ready	Moves to the foredeck		Eases the kicking strap
2 Bears away to a run	Passes the jib sheet over the spinnaker pole. Determines the speed of the gybe for the whole team	Trims the spinnaker for the run. Pulls down twinning line	Eases spinnaker pole downhaul
3 Maintains course in relation to the wind, trying to keep spinnaker drawing	Faces the spinnaker pole, unhooks inboard end, releases guy. Clips pole on to new guy. Checks jib sheet is passed over the pole	Trims spinnaker guy and sheet to keep spinnaker flat	Centres mainsheet traveller and sheets in main to soften the gybe
4 Holds course, keeping spinnaker drawing	Pushes pole hard forward after clipping it on to mast	Swings the spinnaker round the forestay. Lets off twinning line, eases guy as required, then eases sheet	Sheets in mainsail
5 Bears away a few degrees to bring mainsail over on to the new tack	Comes into the cockpit, tightens pole downhaul	Adjusts spinnaker trim to the course being sailed, adjusts twinning line	Frees mainsheet and traveller
6 Luffs gradually on to new course	Tightens kicking strap and sorts out sheets	Fine-trims spinnaker	Adjusts mainsail trim according to heading

Chinese gybe. With the kicking strap insufficiently tensioned, the end of the boom can rear up. The bottom half of the sail is then free to gybe, while the top half catches a spreader, or a batten catches under a shroud. There is a good chance of tearing the sail. The only remedy is to gybe back again quickly so as to get the sail all on one side.

Broach after gybing. This can happen after a planned gybe or an accidental gybe, if the mainsheet is jammed at all (for instance by someone standing on it). It also happens if the helm fails to compensate for the boat's movement, or simply if a large wave catches you unawares.

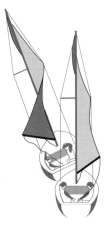

Chinese gybe

Gybing an asymmetric spinnaker

An asymmetric spinnaker is rigged like a genoa, in theory, with sheets to both sides from the single clew, and is carried on the reach. However, in racing fast boats, it can be necessary to gybe the asymmetric spinnaker as you round a mark, since the apparent wind can move round from 90° on one tack to 90° on the other. The only difficulty in gybing can arise if there is too narrow a gap between the forestay and the luff of the sail: the tack should be allowed to blow some way out as the sail is gybed.

Gybing after failing to tack

There are two circumstances in which you might decide to gybe when a tack would be the normal method of going about: either you have just failed to tack and you have not got enough space to leeward of your normal close-hauled course to try again; or you are certain that if you tried again you would fail anyway. The gybe is a sort of last resort in these cases, but it is better to use a last resort quickly than none at all…

If your boat has just failed to tack it will be stopped, facing across the wind, with the sails flogging. Even if you bore away quickly to this position, say, by backing the jib, you can go no further without building up some speed first. The sails are therefore pulled in for the beam reach (the jib can happily be a little oversheeted and the main still a little slack). As you bear away, you can let the sails out slowly in order to keep accelerating.

As you get close to the run, you start to sheet in the main quite fast. You might not be able to pull it all the way in before gybing, if your boat is highly manoeuvrable, but the further in it is by the time the gybe takes place, the better it is.

Once the sail has passed over the centreline of the boat, the sheet

77

needs to be let out quickly. Even if you are aiming to luff up immediately after the gybe, it is best to centre the tiller for a few moments then luff up; otherwise the controlled luff could turn into an uncontrolled broach. You must also ensure that the jib is not let out on one side without being sheeted in on the other; otherwise the clew can catch on the forestay. If the gybe is proving at all difficult, this little extra snag is one you do not need.

As you will already have noticed, the whole procedure for gybing feels different from a tack. When you are going into a tack, success depends to a large extent on the amount of energy and momentum you can muster to throw the boat through the eye of the wind. With a gybe, on the other hand, it is not a question of whether or not the boat will turn, but of whether you can make it do so while retaining the most delicate control.

The only thing you need be uncertain about when gybing is how long the manoeuvre will take to complete: will the spinnaker behave itself; will we be able to avoid broaching and breaking something?

There is no harm in looking briefly at the different risks associated with going about or gybing, depending on whether you are close to land or well out to sea.

Out at sea, failing to tack is no great problem: you have plenty of space to play with and simply need to start over again. In a fresh wind, gybing is perhaps the riskier option, since there is a greater chance of breaking something, which can be unpleasant a long way from harbour.

Closer to land, the opposite is the case. Failing to tack can leave you with little room for a new attempt, and can put you in a difficult situation. It is often wiser to gybe round: if there is too much wind, drop the spinnaker; if there is still too much wind, then simply drop the main, and you will be able to gybe round easily. You should not be embarrassed to adopt such solutions. Old sailors have hundreds of them at their disposal, and do not hesitate to use them.

CHAPTER

3

SAIL HANDLING

We have already looked at some of the alterations to sail trim and shape which are necessary as a result of changes in the weather or the course to be sailed.

Altering the sails in the ways covered so far is an aspect of sail handling. You need to be able to carry out the various routines involved just as smoothly as any change of course. Some of the alterations mean you have to slow the boat down, such as when you change sails or take in a reef; others, such as hoisting the spinnaker, roller-reefing or unreefing the jib, should not slow you down at all. However, any of them can cause chaos aboard the boat if you fail to carry them out precisely and with great attention to detail.

In matters of changing sail, everything depends crucially on details. It is extraordinary how the smallest detail can cause the greatest bother if not attended to properly.

Sail handling usually involves handling cloth in conditions which can be fairly difficult. The fate of the sails hangs literally by a thread: you can lose a jib simply because you omitted to attach one of the hanks to the guardrail, or you can tear the mainsail if you forget to free off a single reefing pennant.

Sail handling includes dropping and hoisting the sails, flattening them, sheeting in quickly. Although every one of these operations is basically simple, they can all cause major problems if certain rules are not adhered to. Ignoring the rules can ultimately incapacitate the boat.

Most of this chapter is devoted to describing the operations involved with sail handling, but you should also read it as a sort of manual of sail care and sail use. We analyse in detail what you need to do to carry out a given operation, without wrecking your sail wardrobe.

Whatever operation you are engaged in, there are a few principles which should be borne in mind:

You should aim to leave the boat minus its sail for the shortest time possible. Some crews, after a lot of practice, can change a jib or take in a reef in under a minute, or set the spinnaker in ten seconds. One should not be over-hasty and run the risk of hoisting the jib upside down, trawling the spinnaker or tying a reefing pennant around a control line.

Whenever the sea is at all rough, every crew member should be clipped on with a safety harness. This is the only legitimate circumstance under which you can ignore the old dictum of 'one hand for you, one for the ship'. With the harness line clipped on, you can use both hands without fear of falling in.

The time and place for the operation should be consciously chosen, wherever possible. The boat loses power when it has less sail up than usual, particularly on the beat, and it slows down and starts to make leeway. You should therefore ensure that there is free water to leeward.

The operation should always be carried out in the same order, and every crew member must know the routine. The operation should be begun only when everyone is ready.

Remember that even simple operations become more difficult and more delicate, the stronger the wind is.

We shall now look in detail at some of the more widely used systems for sail handling. There is not space to look at the most up-to-date designs, which will in any case change annually and are often specific to one design of boat. We shall also describe basic touches which can be carried out without specific gear and which can be used in emergency on any boat.

The jib

As far as foresails are concerned, modern-day boats can be divided into two types:

■ those which have several jibs, each of which serves a specific windspeed range: when there is a change in the wind, you simply swap jibs;

■ those which only have one, all-purpose foresail, which is reefed to a greater or lesser extent to reduce the surface area.

Preparing to change jibs

Jibs can be dropped or hoisted on any point of sailing, but it is easier off the wind for various reasons: the foredeck is then less cluttered with flapping sails and clews with murderous intent; there is no risk of the halyard catching in the spreaders; and it is less hard work pulling the jib up tight and sheeting it in. Finally, if there is a bit of a swell, the foredeck hand is less likely to get soaked than on a beat...

For all these reasons, if you face a long downwind leg with a jib which you know is too large for the beat which follows, you are well advised to swap jibs before luffing up on to the beat. This advice is given as part of our energy-conservation campaign.

How you change jibs depends on how the boat is equipped.

Some cruisers are equipped with two of everything: forestay, halyard and sheets. This is excessive. If we are being selective:

■ a double forestay is utterly indefensible: it is impractical, since the jib hanks always get caught between the stays; and it is even theoretically problematic, since the two forestays can never be maintained at the same tension.

■ two tack attachments are worth having, since they can be arranged simply and cheaply, and they ease the changeover noticeably. It would be silly not to use this device.

■ using two halyards is acceptable, though there can be a risk of confusion;

■ two pairs of sheets can be useful.

In reality, the more equipment you have, the less quickly you can sort things out. A tidy foredeck is the best guarantee you can have that any operation will be carried out quickly and efficiently.

Changing jibs

Getting the new jib ready

Small jibs, up to 20 or 30sq m (200–300 sq ft) are normally stowed in a bag, with the tack at the top. The bag is taken on to the deck and the tack attached to the stem fitting. (If you have only a single fixing point for the jib tack, then you clip the bottom hank to the forestay.)

The bag is then brought back into the cockpit, so that the jib is fed out along the sidedeck, saving time and energy.

Having two tack attachments simplifies matters considerably.

The next step is to clip all the hanks on to the forestay at the bottom, and unclip any you can reach of the current jib hanks.

If the jib is large, it will in any case have been flaked away in a long sausage-shaped sail bag. The bag is placed along the side rail and the tack of the sail is attached. The bag can either be clipped to the rail or removed below, depending on the system.

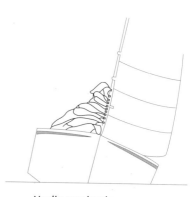

Getting the sheets ready

The sheets should be led through the fairleads before the jib is hoisted, if

Unclip any hanks you can reach of the jib that is set. This gives you more space to hank on the new jib.

83

■

How to use the winch correctly

Almost all winches turn clockwise. (If your winch turns anti-clockwise, the ratchet has been set up wrongly.) The sheet which needs to be winched in is therefore fed on to the winch in the same direction.

Theoretically, the more turns you make on the winch, the less effort is needed on the rope end in your hand. It makes no difference to the winch handle, however. If there are too many turns, they can jam, with the bottom turn riding up on the others such that you cannot free off the top turn.

If this happens, it can cause serious accidents, so you should approach the use of any winch with this in mind. Do not use more turns than you need.

Sheet winches

■ Start by pulling in most of the sheet slack, without using the winch;
■ when virtually all the slack has been taken up, give the sheet a single turn around the winch and keep hauling in;
■ once it starts to become really difficult to pull in, give it a second turn. When you can pull no further by hand, insert the handle into the winch;
■ when the turns slip over the winch drum, make yet another turn;
■ keep going, using up to four or five turns if necessary;
■ as soon as you see the bottom turn riding over the next, let the sheet out slightly by allowing the turns to slip with your hand as you continue using the handle (this is particularly important if you are using a self-tailing winch);
■ in order to free the sheet from the winch, simply pull the sheet vertically upwards from the drum.

possible, so as to leave the boat underpowered for the shortest possible time. This can be done in a number of ways:

■ if the same sheets are used for each jib, in the same fairleads, there is nothing to change;
■ if the same sheets are used but led through different fairleads, then you can use the windward sheet of the old jib as the leeward sheet of the new one;
■ if the new jib has its own sheets attached, then they can be put in place immediately.

If the fairleads have no room for two sheets at the same time, you simply have to wait and put the sheets in position all at the same time.

Dropping the jib

One crew member lets the jib down, using the halyard which is normally made off to port. If you are sailing downwind, it is best to cleat the sheet in, to prevent the jib falling in the water. If you are on a beat, you might have to ease the sheet a little so that the hanks slide down the forestay more easily.

This works even on winches with a top-fitting handle (so long as the handle is removable).

Halyard winches

- Start by pulling the sail up without using the winch;
- as the sail reaches the top, put a few turns on the winch, then continue adding turns (as for the sheet winch) as the resistance increases;
- the sail can be at the top between ratchet clicks: you therefore continue turning the handle without pulling on the halyard tail, thus allowing the next ratchet tooth to engage;
- a halyard winch is freed in the same way as a sheet winch.

Important precaution

Do not touch a sheet which is between the winch and the sail. Any slight slackening of the sheet as it comes on to the winch drum encourages riding turns. You might not even notice this happen (especially at night), and you can then find yourself suddenly unable to free the sheet or halyard when you need to tack or lower the sail.

Bringing the halyard into the cockpit

These days, most halyards are led back into the cockpit. Pulling the sail up from inside the cockpit demands a lot of strength, and the problem is generally dealt with by using two people. One hoists the sail, standing at the bottom of the mast, while the other takes up the slack and then winches from inside the cockpit.

You can end up with a real bird's nest of halyards in the cockpit. To avoid this, the halyard should be stowed neatly in a small bag which is hung up by the steps to the cabin or put in a safe place on the floor.

The foredeck hand should try to pull the jib down as quickly as possible to limit the amount of time it spends flogging. Stopping it from falling in the water is useful but of secondary importance: the sail will not dissolve in salt water.

Changing the three corners

As soon as the jib is down, the halyard end must be cleated. The heads of the two sails should then be brought together and the halyard shackle transferred from one to the other.

You need to pay attention at this stage. If it takes any time at all to transfer the halyard from one jib head to the other, the boat's natural movement will be enough to wrap the halyard round the forestay. You will not always notice this happening, especially at night. The infuriating thing is that you can usually still pull the jib up, but after a couple more hours' sailing, the wire part of the halyard will be ready for the dustbin.

The old jib hanks need to be taken off the forestay (and care needs to be taken not to take off the new hanks!). If you keep one arm between the forestay and the halyard you can spot your mistake

85

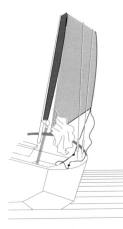

A: The windward sheet is taken from the old jib to be used as the leeward sheet on the new one.

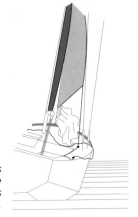

B: The new jib sheets are put in place before the old jib is dropped.

quickly enough. Do make sure there are still one or two hanks of the old jib attached to the forestay before you detach the tack, if you are operating on a single stem fitting, or you might lose the jib overboard. Change the sheets over from one jib to the other, and slide the fairlead along its track if necessary.

Hoisting, stretching and trimming the jib

The crew member who hoists the sail also stretches the luff and makes the halyard off. As this is going on, someone else needs to sheet the jib in a little to stop it from flogging. The jib is sheeted in properly only after the halyard has been cleated.

Headfoils

The same procedure is used when the jib luff runs inside a headfoil, except that there are no hanks. The jib is slightly harder to drop and hoist because there is greater friction, and it is not always easy to guide the luff rope into the headfoil groove. The only real problem is the halyard: if you wrap the halyard around the foil at any stage, the foil can become bent. If this happens, either it becomes impossible to pull the jib up any further, or – which is worse – the jib goes up easily enough but will not come down.

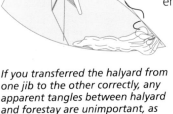

If you have a headfoil with twin grooves, you can hoist one jib before dropping the other. This operation can be difficult, because the two sails rub against each other as well as in the groove. It is really only possible in light winds.

If you transferred the halyard from one jib to the other correctly, any apparent tangles between halyard and forestay are unimportant, as they will unwrap themselves automatically as the jib is hoisted.

Who does what: changing foresails

Phase	Helm	Crew 1	Crew 2	Crew 3
1	Steers a constant course (avoiding close-hauled if possible)	Attaches new jib to forestay between tack and lowest hank of old jib		Positions windward jib fairlead
2	Maintains course	Shackles windward sheet to clew of new jib	Prepares jib halyard and awaits the next order	
3	Maintains course	Gives the order to drop the jib when ready, and bundles the old jib on the foredeck	Uncleats and releases jib halyard	
4	Maintains course	Shackles halyard to head of new jib, swaps tack		
5	Maintains course	Shackles new sheet on		Positions leeward jib fairlead
6	Maintains course	Unhanks old jib		Fetches bag for old jib
7	Maintains course	Hands old jib to Crew 3 for stowing		Stows old jib in its bag, making sure the three corners are uppermost
8	Maintains course	Hoists new jib quickly from mast foot	Helps Crew 1, taking up any slack	
9	Maintains course		Adjusts halyard tension and jib camber according to wind strength	Trims new jib

Roller-reefing gear means that the crew does not need to venture onto the foredeck.

Furling the jib

This operation is as simple as it sounds. The jib should already be flat, as you tightened the luff when the wind freshened, so you simply need to pull in the furling line, letting the sheet out as necessary while you are furling (not too fast, or the sail will flap), then sheeting in again once you have reduced the sail area to the desired extent.

Even with a jib which is rigged on a roller-reefing attachment, the all-purpose jib is never quite that. Even the most carefully made all-purpose jib will be either a little too flat for light airs or too full for heavy winds. As a compromise, too flat is preferable to too full.

Raising the storm jib

The storm jib is an absolute must on board. You need to give particular attention to arrangements for its use.

A storm jib designed to be used with a headfoil is pointless. The purpose of having such a sail on board is for when your normal system is broken or unusable, in an emergency.

The storm jib should not be hoisted using only its own luff rope. You should therefore have an emergency wire stay, preferably one which is fitted to the mast and shackled down to a padeye on the foredeck when it is needed. If you have not got such a stay, then a normal halyard can be used, but the storm jib must have a wire or Kevlar luff if it is to be tensioned sufficiently.

It is worth having a second jib halyard, especially if the jib uses furling gear: if something goes wrong with furling gear, it can be very difficult to recover the halyard out at sea.

Tidying up

Lead the windward sheet through its fairlead if you have space.

Stow the jib away

Small jibs are stowed in a bag, according to a precise routine: first the head is put away, then the sail is fed into the bag so that the tack is uppermost, this being the part to which you will need most immediate access next time you use the sail.

Large jibs are flaked and tied in a sausage shape along the side deck then put away (either in their long sail bag or straight down the

■

Old sailors' tricks

Changing jibs is a wet, tiring and occasionally dangerous job. You can make your life simpler as follows:

On the beat Drop the jib just as the tack com-
mences (or just as soon as you are sure the boat has
passed head to wind, if there is a fresh breeze, to
avoid any risk of failing the tack), and hoist the new
jib after the tack.

An alternative method is to sit with the wind on
the beam and the mainsail just tight enough to
avoid flogging. This makes the foredeck rather
drier and safer, at the expense of losing some
ground to windward.

Downwind The new jib can be positioned on
the windward side,
the old one dropped
and then the boat
gybed. The new jib is
hoisted after the
gybe.

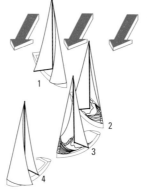

*1 The new jib is
prepared to windward.
2 The old jib is
dropped before the
gybe.
3 The boat gybes.
4 The new jib is
hoisted on the new
tack.*

*The new jib is set
up to windward.
The old jib is
dropped as you
tack, and the
new one hoisted
once you are on
the new tack.*

fore hatch) clew first, so that you have immediate access to the tack
next time you want to use the sail.

The mainsail

Mainsails are generally less easy to handle than jibs. You cannot drop
the sail or hoist it on every point of sailing; keeping the boat on
course with no mainsail is a tricky business; and as the weather dete-
riorates and you need to reduce the amount of sail set, you are more
likely to roll the sail or reef it than to swap it over. (You will not usually have two mainsails anyway.)

Although changing or reducing the mainsail is not complicated,
there is a right way to do it, and we shall study that in detail once we
have dealt with some general principles.

Hoisting and dropping the mainsail

The wind must be forward of the beam. In order for the sail to slide **89** along the mast track, it needs to be more or less along the centreline of the boat, not resting on the rigging. This is generally possible only somewhere between a close reach and head to wind. Even with the wind on the beam the slides are under too much sideways stress and will jam in the mast track.

The jib can be very handy as the mainsail is being raised or dropped: if it is slightly over-sheeted, it can backwind the main, thus allowing you to keep working even with the wind on the beam and even if the topmast shrouds are fixed to the deck aft of the mast.

The boom must be supported, at least during two stages of the operation: when you are finishing hoisting the sail or beginning to let it down. If you do not support the boom, the sail stretches the luff rope at an angle and pulls it out either at the tack or at the top slide. This is a good way of stretching your sail permanently out of shape, tearing it, losing a slide or bending the track.

The usual way of supporting the boom is to let the kicking strap off and use the topping lift. Smaller boats will not have a topping lift, so a member of the crew supports the boom by hand. In order for that person to reach the boom, it needs to be central, so the boat has to be close-hauled. The person supporting the boom needs to be to leeward and fairly well forward: if they stay too far aft or in the middle of the boat, they will not have a good angle of purchase on the boom.

Ways of reducing sail
There are two alternative systems for reducing the mainsail area: reefs and furlers.

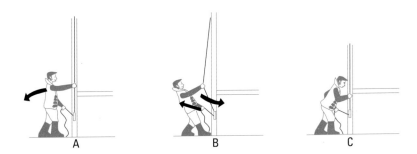

A   B   C

Sweating the halyard up without a winch
Anyone can get the halyard as tight as a harp string, but not everyone succeeds in stretching the luff correctly. Once the sail is up to the top, the halyard should be led under the cleat and held steady in your left hand. You can then steady yourself against the mast foot and take hold of the halyard at shoulder height with one hand, leaning back to tension it. The halyard can then be pulled down the mast with a strong downward tug, while you take up the slack with the other hand.

■ Reefing is the traditional way of reducing the area of the mainsail. The reefing points run in lines along the sail, with bands hanging down either side from reinforcing patches. When you need to reduce the sail area, you fold that part of the sail between the boom and the reefing points over on itself, tying the reefing points around and under the boom.

Reefing has one major shortcoming: since there are only a few rows of reefing points, you always have to take away a large and invariable part of the sail area. On occasion, this will be more than you want to reduce. It is easy, however, to keep the sail in good shape so that it continues to draw well. The operation is simple and involves no machinery, so it cannot break down.

■ Mainsail furling involves furling the sail inside the mast or boom in much the same way as a jib furler works.

Furling appears quick and easy, and it is fair to say that it does have certain advantages over traditional slab reefing: you can reduce sail by exactly the desired amount, and you do not have to be close-hauled to carry the operation out. However, mainsail furlers are a relatively recent invention, and it is early yet to judge the complete balance of their advantages and disadvantages. Certainly, if you are equipped with furling gear, there is no harm in having reefing points as well, as a second line of defence!

The oldest method of reducing sail was to roll it around the boom. This method has died out these days because it makes it difficult to keep the sail in good shape.

Reefing

You need to arrange your working conditions so as to ensure a quick and efficient reefing procedure.

The boom needs to be well supported and the sail must not be drawing. The best course to sail is thus a close reach or close fetch.

Maintaining course

The helm's job is simply to keep the boat on course, without bothering about speed or sideways drift. If the boat is kept well on course, it will barely move forward at all and the reef can be taken in an instant.

Some people recommend trying to keep the boat heading in the same direction throughout by heaving to (backing the jib), but in our experience this does not really work. The only way for the boat to keep its heading is for the mainsail to draw…

Since it is impossible to tension the foot if the mainsail is allowed to draw all the time, you have to steer a middle course, not allowing the sail to draw all the time, but just giving it enough power to keep the boat heading up.

Necessary precautions

The sail must not be allowed to flap hard or for long. Flapping deforms the leech, and can even cause battens to break and tear the cloth. This is one reason to get the reef over with quickly. (The sail will flap harder as you are carrying out the reef if the leech is under too much tension, so you should ensure you release it using the topping lift.)

It is not usually necessary to take the bottom batten out, unless through some design fault its pocket is at the same height as the reefing points.

Keeping the sail shape

A sail which sets well despite the reduction in area is a major advantage to anyone trying to sail in heavy winds. As we noted above, keeping a good shape to the sail is one of the major advantages of reefing; and it is possible to get a perfectly shaped sail if you adjust the tack, clew and reefing pennants properly.

The tack should be as close as possible to the gooseneck. This is usually accomplished by a simple hook.

The clew should be held down on the boom if possible. It should not be pulled too far aft, however. The important issue is to control the foot tension: if there is too much, the sail creases along the foot at the reefing points; and if there is too little, the reefing points themselves carry too much of the load and might tear. The foot tension is what controls the shape of the sail, so you need to find a good medium setting.

The clew is usually pulled down with a pennant, which will be designed so that the reefing operation works quickly and easily, and also so that you can control the foot tension precisely.

The reefing points hold down the folded part of the sail. Ideally, they should pass between the foot rope and the boom, if the foot is on a slide track, as this gives a better 'grip' on the sail. If the foot is fed along a groove, they will have to be knotted around under the boom. This allows the sailcloth to slip around, and can easily rub against the shroud when you are on a run. (This is another good reason for tying that figure-of-eight knot in the mainsheet just below the bottom block, so that the sail and boom do not come into contact with the shrouds.)

Most modern sails have a high aspect ratio, and a relatively short boom. The function of the reefing points is thus largely one of keeping the sail tidy. It is possible to sail without knotting the points, even if the aesthetic and aerodynamic effect is unfortunate. With a relatively long boom, the reefing points help to keep the sail flat (though they should not be used on their own to flatten a sail with a loose foot).

Taking in a reef

There are many reefing systems, each one more ingenious than the other. Many of them work very well. The method we shall describe here uses the most widespread system, with hooks at the tack and reefing pennants through the boom.

The tack hook
The hook is very simple to use: it might need to be cleaned, but the only real mistake would be to fit the sail cringle over it upside down.

The clew pennants
The reefing pennant is run along inside the boom, with a figure-of-eight knot at the end. The aft end of the pennant is fed through the clew reefing cringle and fastened to a slider on the boom. (If there is no slider, the pennant is led under the boom and tied to itself with a bowline between the cringle and the end of the boom.) This operation should be completed before you let the sail down, so that you do not have to go to the end of the boom again. If you feed the pennant through later, the reef will take longer and be more difficult. It is common practice to keep the lower pennant permanently reeved, which is not a problem provided that the tension is adjusted each time the mainsail is hoisted.

Lowering the sail
Come on to a close reach or close fetch. Let out the mainsail and the kicking strap and support the boom at about 30° above the horizontal. Let the halyard down just enough to be able to fit the tack cringle over the hook.

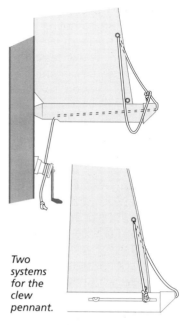

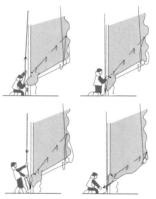

Two systems for the clew pennant.

Ready to take in the reef...
1 Take the strain on the topping lift. Let down as much mainsail as needed, taking out any slides from the mast track if necessary.
2 Fit the tack cringle over the hook the right way up.
3 Sweat the mainsail back up.
4 Tighten the clew reef pennant, then wait for the right moment to finish off with the reefing points. Then, you just let off the topping lift, sheet in, tighten the kicker and back on course.

■

If the clew pennant...

... is not put in place before you let the sail down, the procedure takes longer, and in the following order:

■ ease the mainsheet and kicking strap,
■ support the boom slightly,
■ drop the sail by two reefs,
■ sheet in and cleat the mainsheet,

■ reeve the pennant through,
■ ease the sheet,
■ support the boom at 30°
■ fit the tack cringle over the hook.

Taking in the reef

■ Hook the tack cringle on at the gooseneck, ensuring that the sail is not twisted;

■ pull the sail back up and cleat the halyard;

■ pull the clew pennant tight and adjust the foot tension. This can only be done if the boom is thoroughly supported. You have to choose your moment for tightening the pennant, and maybe help the pennant into place at the boom end as you are tightening it.

Starting off again

Ease the topping lift, pull the sail in, tighten the kicking strap and start back on your course.

Checking the sail

If the reef curves markedly out from the boom, you have not put on enough foot tension. If the reef is lying dead flat along the boom, the foot is too tight. A happy medium is for the reefed sail to bulge out from the boom at the middle by about 3 per cent–5 per cent of the foot length. Adjusting the foot tension is relatively simple, though you need to let the sheet off while you do so.

Furling the loose sailcloth

Bring the boat on to a close-hauled course so that all the foot of the sail is within reach. All the loose sail which will not be used should be pulled down and rolled into itself tightly. Tie the reef points in a bow.

If you need to sail some course other than a beat, then the reefing bands should be left untied for the time being. This is not too inconvenient.

The only thing left to do is to tighten the kicking strap.

Most prudent sailors now reeve the second pennant.

Although the operation may appear long, as described above, it can be carried out with a practised crew so as to leave you without the mainsail for little more than half a minute, during which time the boat will not have moved far at all.

If you need to take your time about taking in the reef (for

instance when the crew is tired) then you can simply drop the whole sail while doing it. It has to be said that there are few advantages to doing this unless the boat is sailing a course very far off the wind and there is little chance of the boat rolling dangerously in the swell. If you do drop the main, you should take particular care to ensure all the reefing points used are in the same row; it is also very easy to tie the mainsheet, the guardrails, the lifebelt and any other nearby pieces of rope in with the reefing points.

One final detail: if the breeze has really freshened very suddenly, you may need to take in a double reef in one go. If you have sufficient time (and sufficient water to leeward), it is actually better to take in the first reef and then the second, rather than going straight for the second. Otherwise, when the wind moderates again, you will have to let go of everything in order to take in the first reef then.

Shaking out a reef

This is a simple and quick operation. There are a few necessary precautions, the most important of which is making sure that you have actually untied all the reefing points before you do anything else. One crew member carries the job out, and another must follow, checking everything is free. No one should resent having their work checked in this manner: it is so easy and so disastrous to miss one, that the whole boat and crew might suffer to save the pride of one person.

■

Taking in a reef without special systems, or after a gear breakage

For this technique to work:
- ■ the boom must be inboard;
- ■ the sail must not be drawing.

This means staying on a close-hauled heading with the mainsail eased throughout.

The procedure is:
- ■ to come up to close-hauled;
- ■ to lower the main a long way, as if for two reefs;
- ■ to cleat the mainsheet so as to immobilise the boom (to make sure it does not knock anyone overboard);
- ■ to fasten the tack down;
- ■ to tension the foot;
- ■ free the sheet;
- ■ to tighten the topping lift and rehoist the sail;
- ■ to sheet in and take up your original course again.

95

The reef is shaken out on a beat. The rest of the operation is:

■ letting off the kicking strap;

■ supporting the boom;

■ letting off the clew pennant; freeing the tack cringle;

■ feeding the slides into the mast track;

■ hauling the sail up and cleating the halyard, tightening the kicking strap and setting off again;

■ stow carefully the reefing pennants.

If you have no topping lift, remember to support the boom as you release the clew pennant, or the boom will crash on to the deck.

Changing mainsails

At sea

This operation can take ten to twenty minutes in fresh winds, even with a modest-sized sail. The boat needs to be close-hauled for dropping and hauling the sail up; but once the main is lying on the deck, there is no need to prevent the boat bearing away naturally.

The main problem in this operation is to get a clear view of what is going on. You should only have one sail on the deck at a time, and the change sail should be correctly furled so that it is easily slipped on to the boom without needing to be unfolded.

A mainsail really needs to be furled with the foot straight and the luff rope folded in concertina fashion down to it. It is not possible to make a good job of this afloat: it needs to be done on land, where you can prevent the wind blowing the sail about.

Afloat, then, you need a simple short-cut. You fold the foot up to about half the height of the first reef to make it into a pocket, then drop the rest of the sail into the pocket in as regular a manner as you can manage, taking the battens out as you fold in the sail. Close the pocket around the sail and tie it together.

In port

In port, if you want to leave the sail along the boom, you can make it into a pocket in the same way and fold in the sail, leaving the battens in place and any slides still in the mast track. It is vital the sail is packed tightly so as not to rub and wear itself out. The halyard should also be tight (though not pulling the sail up), so it needs to be made off on an appropriate fitting on the mast or elsewhere, or at least hooked on somewhere if you leave it shackled to the headboard.

The furled sail can be tied up either with a series of independent sail ties, with shock cords or in a chain knot using a few of the reefing pennants. There are two methods of tying the sail which cannot be recommended: using the mainsheet means you cannot change the position of the boom without undoing the whole lot; and using any sort of double chain knot means it will become slack as time goes on.

The spinnaker

The spinnaker (or 'kite', to the initi-
ated), started life as a racing sail, and
this racing pedigree is apparent in
the way it is used even in cruising
yachts. It is a minor aristocrat
among sails, and needs to be
pampered and attended to
during its unique operations;
nor can it stand waiting
around at anything less
than full power once it is
up. Sailors of little faith
speak of their spin-
nakers as being con-
trary, whereas in
reality they are just
spirited, like
highly strung
racehorses.
Certainly their
retainers can
get a nasty

Spinnaker equipment

shock at the ease with which the aristocratic sail turns ill-tempered.

We have already studied the handling of the spinnaker once it is
up, and looked at how to gybe it. However, hoisting and dropping
the spinnaker are subjects worthy of study in their own right, as
these stages (at least initially) are among the most problematic
aspects of spinnaker handling.

The sail

Early racing spinnakers looked rather like two staysails sewn together
at the luff. Over the years, the sail has become fuller and the edges
more rounded, so that what we have nowadays is like a rather bul-
bous isosceles triangle which is vertically symmetrical.

The top corner of the sail (which can make any angle up to 180°)
is the head. The two bottom corners are known alternately as the
tack and clew, depending on whether they are to windward or to
leeward. They make an angle of around 135°. The windward edge of
the sail is the luff and the leeward edge the leech; the bottom edge
is known as the foot.

Spinnakers come in all shapes and sizes. They are made of more
or less light cloths, depending on the wind strength for which they
are designed. A reaching spinnaker can be carried even on quite a
close reach, and has to be flatter than a running spinnaker. In the

97

same way, cruising spinnakers tend to be flatter and heavier than racing spinnakers.

The rigging

Spinnaker rigging consists essentially of:

■ the halyard, led through a block or sheave above the forestay. The bottom end of the halyard is usually made off at the port side of the mast foot, like the jib halyard, back to the cockpit to avoid mix-ups;

■ two ropes (called collectively 'sheets'), one on either of the bottom corners, for trimming and directing the spinnaker; like the corners themselves, the ropes change name depending on whether they are to windward (the guy) or to leeward (the sheet). Both are led aft to fairleads as far aft as possible and outboard. They need winches for controlling them, and should be about twice as long as the boat itself.

Some boats use double sheets on both sides;

■ a pole which holds the tack out from the mast; the tip of the pole which is next to the mast may be called the heel, while the other is just known as the end. Fast multihulls are generally wide enough not to need a pole. On small boats, the ends of the pole are usually identical, so either end can be used as the heel; on larger boats the ends tend to be different, and there will usually be a track slider and uphaul/downhaul system on the front of the mast so that the heel can be set at different heights;

■ a pole uphaul, which supports the pole and allows you to raise the outer end. This will be fixed either in the middle of the pole (on small boats) or at the outer end (on larger boats);

■ a pole downhaul, which prevents the pole end from skying. On small boats, the downhaul goes from the middle of the pole to the mast foot, so the pole angle can be changed without changing the downhaul setting. On larger boats, the downhaul goes from the end of the pole to the bow; any change in the pole angle thus means that you have also to alter the downhaul setting.

On many boats, all the controls for the spinnaker are led back to the cockpit, so that it is possible to trim it entirely without sending anyone up onto the foredeck.

Rigging the spinnaker

All the control lines for the spinnaker (guy and sheet, uphaul and downhaul, etc.) are generally left in place whether the sail is up or not. The sail is brought on to the deck only when you are just about to set it.

Preparing the sail

As a rule, the spinnaker is made ready down in the calm of the

Sorting the spinnaker out with the bottomless bucket

cabin. (No smoking or cooking is allowed while this is going on.)

The first question is whether you are going to furl it or not. This is seldom absolutely necessary, though it is sensible in certain circumstances, such as when the jib is down, or if you plan to hoist the sail up while you are pulling the guy at the same time. (We shall return to this 'quick' method later on.) It is usually worth keeping the jib up, even if that means some of the operations become more complicated: the jib prevents the spinnaker filling before you have got it fully hoisted, and, most crucially, stops the spinnaker from wrapping itself round the forestay.

Whether you elect to furl the spinnaker or not, one of the most practical ways of getting the spinnaker ready is to use a bucket with the bottom cut out of it. (Any other rigid ring of about the same diameter will work just as well.) You pull the sail through the hole, head first, guiding the edges of the sail in and making sure they do not twist over each other, all the way down to the bottom corners. You then take a turtle and pack the sail into it, starting with the cloth which has not been through the bucket, keeping the bottom corners out of the turtle and well apart; this process is continued until you have pulled all the sail back through the bucket and into the turtle, keeping an eye on the edges of the sail as you go.

The head of the sail is kept out of the bag and between the two bottom corners.

If you intend to hoist the spinnaker in stops, then the preparations have to be made as the spinnaker comes through the bucket the first time. You tie thin strands of cotton or wool around the sail, which are designed to break as soon as you tighten the guy and sheet. The top tie must be two metres or so beneath the head, as it will not break if it is higher up. Rubber bands work equally well.

Novice crews or those who have few spare hands are recommended to use a spinnaker sock. This is a long thin bag, the length of the spinnaker sides. The bottom end has a rigid ring built in it; the top end has a snapshackle on the inside which can be attached

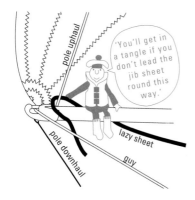

'You'll get in a tangle if you don't lead the jib sheet round this way.'

pole uphaul

pole downhaul

lazy sheet

guy

99

to the head of the sail, and a ring on the outside which the halyard is passed through.

There is an uphaul-downhaul system for raising the bag up above the sail once it has been hoisted, by pulling the ring up, and dropping it down over the sail to refurl it before you strike it.

The bag is placed and tied at the aft end of the foredeck, ideally just in front of the shrouds. This is an important detail, as it ensures the spinnaker is hoisted in the wind shadow of the mainsail and will not fill until you guy the pole into place.

Preparing the rigging

You must keep a keen eye on every rope and the course you are asking it to take. The whole stage must be perfectly set before you dare raise the curtain. The skipper must take time to examine everyone's work and check that the diagrams below have been followed in the minutest detail.

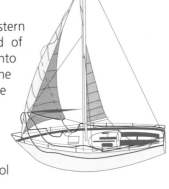

The skipper's checklist
Windward side:

■ the guy should come from the stern outside everything, through the end of the pole, in front of the forestay and into the spinnaker tack, passing over the guardrails, under the jib and under the windward jib sheet;

■ the downhaul comes from the end of the pole, over the guardrails, then through its block into the cockpit, underneath all the other control lines and sheets.

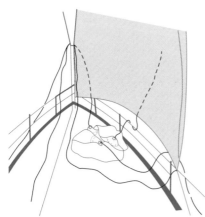

Another way of keeping the windward jib sheet untangled.

Leeward side:

■ the sheet should come from the stern outside everything and be attached to the clew, passing over the rails, under the jib and the leeward sheet;

■ the halyard is normally made off on the port side, but here it has had to be moved round since the boat is on the port tack, and it would have been on the wrong side of the forestay. It is led around the front of the jib and on to the spinnaker head over the rails, under the jib and under the windward sheet.

The three main ropes attached to the sail are thus fed through the same 'gap' in the boat's rigging to reach the sail.

With the boat set up this way, you are still free to tack if needs be, because you made sure that the windward jib sheet was led over the spinnaker pole.

Final preparations

1 Come on to the correct course, i.e. a beam reach. You should aim not to have to raise the spinnaker on a broad reach or run because then the mainsail and jib make an effective screen which stops the wind filling the spinnaker.

2 Let the mainsail fully out, to prevent the spinnaker coming between the spreaders and the mainsail.

3 Trim and cleat the jib, so it does not get in the way.

4 Let off the pole downhaul.

5 Raise the pole so it is horizontal and pointing straight forward, against the forestay.

6 Do not cleat the sheet! It should be released as the spinnaker is hoisted, so that there is no danger of the spinnaker filling prematurely.

Remember the essential rule: from the moment you start to hoist the spinnaker, *everyone on board must be clipped on.* As soon as you are sailing under spinnaker, it takes at least twice as long to turn the boat round and fish any crew member out of the sea if they fall overboard.

The spinnaker has come out of its bag nicely in the wind shadow of the other sails. The main is well eased so the spinnaker cannot catch on a spreader, and the presence of the jib prevents it from getting wrapped round the forestay. Both the guy and the sheet are slack, so the sail will not fill. What else is there to do but wait?
You now need to adjust the guy and pole, and sheet in.
So long as the sheet is not pulled, the spinnaker will not fill. To stop the spinnaker twisting, the guy is pulled first, so that the tack reaches the end of the pole. The halyard is cleated as soon as the sail is fully hoisted.

101

Hoisting the spinnaker

The sail must be hoisted quickly. If there is a strongish wind, you should take a turn round a winch, so that the crew member who is hoisting the sail does not have their arms pulled out of their sockets if it fills too early. It is helpful for one member of the crew to stand by the turtle and help the sail out of it.

Adjusting the guy

When the halyard has been cleated, pull the guy round so as to position the pole at right angles to the apparent wind.

If the spinnaker will not unfurl, it is probably twisted on itself. This can happen when you put the sail in the turtle, if you hoist it when too far off the wind, if you are slow bringing the tack round to the pole end or if you hoist the sail too slowly.

The spinnaker can often be untwisted before it fills with wind, by a short tug on one edge. If this does not work the first time, it probably will not work the second: then it is better to drop the spinnaker by pulling on the luff, sort it out on the foredeck, then hoist it again. This is faster than trying to sort it out aloft.

Sheeting in

When the pole is in position you can begin to sheet in. There is no great urgency to this: so long as the sheet is not pulled, the spinnaker will not fill. If you are using a sock, this is the moment at which you slip it up to the top and sheet the spinnaker in. Before doing either ensure that the halyard is cleated, as the crew could not possibly hold on to it and rope burns would probably result.

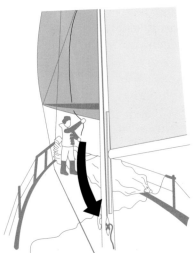

When you have dropped the jib, the first job is to remove the jib halyard from the jib and bring it back to the mastfoot.

Trimming the spinnaker

After a while, you are back on course, so you can begin to adjust the spinnaker to the precise wind and to the course you are sailing.

On a beam reach, you can keep the jib up, which might give a little extra power. An alternative is to use a specialist sail which might be more appropriate, such as a spinnaker staysail.

On a broad reach or a run, the jib gets in the way, so it is better to drop it and hoist the big boy.

Important rule: the jib halyard must not be left along the length of the forestay, because if the spinnaker does collapse and wrap itself between the pair of them, it will be virtually impossible to undo.

The quick method

With a little practice, you can pull the spinnaker up and fill it more quickly; if necessary, you can do this on a pretty close reach.

The spinnaker turtle is tied by the forestay. The tack is pulled up to the pole end just before you start to pull on the halyard, and the pole is guyed round to the correct position. The sail is then pulled up very fast, not forgetting to take a turn on the winch: you need to get the sail up before the wind manages to fill it.

If the sheet is properly eased, this should work smoothly.

Hoist the jib and free the mainsheet.

Dropping the spinnaker

Hoisting the jib

The jib should be hoisted immediately before you drop the spinnaker, so as to take some of the wind out of it and prevent it wrapping round the forestay.

You need to ensure before hoisting the jib that the sheets are well clear of the spinnaker gear, so that the foredeck remains in order.

Let off the guy and let the spinnaker fly out...

Coming on to the right course

Just as when you were hoisting the spinnaker, you should aim for the spinnaker to be in the wind shadow of the mainsail.

The ideal course for dropping the spinnaker is a broad or maybe a beam reach. You should not attempt to drop the spinnaker on a dead run, especially in waves, for fear of accidental gybes.

Once you have mastered the technique, you will find you can drop the spinnaker on any point of sailing, even a beat. You will need to learn to do this as part of the 'man overboard' drill.

... before it subsides gently in the lee of the mainsail, allowing you to bundle it inboard and drop it very easily.

103

Easing the mainsheet

As you drop the spinnaker, you need to increase the size of the mainsail's wind shadow by easing the mainsheet. This also prevents the spinnaker catching on the spreader, if the mainsail is up against it.

Danger

No smoking!

Freeing the tack

The guy should be freed a long way so that the pole is against the forestay with the spinnaker flapping in the lee of the mainsail.

The guy needs to be let off fairly quickly, especially in a fresh breeze, if you are not to broach. Once the pole is against the forestay, the tack snapshackle can be released and the sail is free to come down.

Dropping the spinnaker

Before you drop the spinnaker, you need to be sure it is no longer filling, and is behind the mainsail. If you have a sock, you can let it down at this point, and the operation is complete.

If you have no spinnaker sock, the delicate part of the procedure is letting the halyard off on demand with the crew bundling the sail inboard. The halyard needs to be let down quite slowly.

One or more crew members pull first on the sheet, then on the sail itself, holding either the cloth or one of the edges (though not both, or it will fill again).

The spinnaker can be smothered on the deck, though it is often not keen to lie down, and it is easy for the crew to slip on it. The best thing is to pull it inboard under the boom and take it straight below deck: there it can be packed away in its turtle with the three corners poking out of the top, and the turtle closed. Then it is ready for its next airing.

Making off the halyard

Once the head has been detached from the halyard, the halyard can be clipped on to its usual place at the port side of the foot of the mast. Careful, though, if you pulled it down while on the port tack: the halyard will have to be led back round the forestay before being made fast.

If your halyard is made of rope, it can be clipped on to the bow pulpit, though it will cause some windage there. Wire halyards must under no circumstances be left at the pulpit, as they catch in the jib hanks.

Tidying up

The pole is put back in its place and the downhaul tightened. The sheets are clipped on to the pulpit, tightened aft and held along the outside of the boat with breaking twine if necessary. If you were not prepared to hoist the jib at the beginning of the operation, you can do it now, with everything tidy. The operation is in the bag, as they say…

The quick method

The decision to drop the spinnaker is often made when the wind heads you on a reach and you can no longer sail as high as you would like. Sometimes you even need to drop the spinnaker as you are luffing up, either because the wind has changed, or because you are entering a channel or rounding a mark in a race.

You certainly need to drop the spinnaker in a hurry if someone falls overboard. In such cases, you bring the sail down using a short cut: the guy is completely released, the spinnaker flies out behind the main and you then bundle it inboard hand over hand at the back of the boat and to leeward. The halyard is let down as the sail comes into the boat, and you might find it worth while to take a turn round the winch to stop it coming down too quickly. This emergency method only works if the spinnaker sheets have no figure-of-eight knot in the end, so never tie a figure-of-eight knot in a spinnaker sheet.

This technique, it should be noted, occasionally results in the loss of the guy and its snapshackle.

How much sail can we carry?

A little practice goes a long way to help you change sails efficiently: but you need a lot of experience to decide when and by how much you need to reduce or increase the boat's sail area. You cannot always solve the problem with a rule of thumb along the lines of 'take in the first reef at force 4'. There is an infinite variety of solutions, according to your boat and the conditions obtaining. We can only give a few general hints, returning to points made in earlier chapters.

A boat's performance is partly predetermined by its shape, weight, size and sail design. It can be either 'stiff' or 'tender', i.e. capable of carrying a lot of sail as the wind increases, or needing to reduce sail fairly early. As the wind increases, the boat might develop more or less weather helm on the beat, and roll either more or less on the run. You can get an idea of when to change the sail area from the angle of heel or the degree by which it becomes hard to steer.

To get the right sails for the conditions, you must pay as much attention to the shape of the sails as to their surface area. They should be full in light winds, then progressively flattened as the wind freshens. If the wind is really gusty, you are often best advised to flatten the jib so that it continues to be usable in the gusts, with a fairly full mainsail so that you have some power in the calm patches.

The state of the sea is also an important variable: on a sheltered stretch of sea you might be able to keep all sail on in a given wind, while the same wind on a rough sea would certainly force a reduction on you.

There are also subjective factors to consider: how experienced your crew is, what sort of sailing you are doing. If you are racing, or your crew is keen and eager, your primary concern might well be speed, and any changes you make to the boat's sails will be carried out swiftly and efficiently. You can also look at the problem from the other end: a novice crew should be encouraged to make as many changes as you think prudent, so as to gain confidence and skill. However, if you are cruising, and the crew is inexperienced, of course you will leave a greater margin of security, reducing the sail area earlier, knowing that any operation becomes more difficult when there is more power in the sails; in the same way, you will probably think twice before shaking out a reef or hoisting the spinnaker.

There is no hard and fast rule. At best, there is a basic principle: you need your boat to be manoeuvrable at all times. This means it should have enough power to steer by, but not so much that it is out of balance. Speed is also an element which contributes positively to your safety and comfort, even if you are not competing with anyone. Under-canvassed is no better than over-canvassed: one boat sits upright but does not move, and the other lies on its ear. Neither is a pretty sight.

4

MAN OVERBOARD

This is our final chapter on handling a boat under sail. It is rather different from the previous chapters. Manoeuvring the boat is only a small part of what needs to be done when a crew member falls overboard: we also have to cover prevention techniques, how to lift people out of the sea and any first aid that might be necessary. We have chosen to include all these topics here, although they are not all questions of boat handling, and in part because of the light they throw on the preceding chapters. This chapter shows the difficulty of combining good theory with good practice, and it should serve as a reminder of the need for rigour and crew training in the use of your boat. It is fine to be able to make a boat move, but complete mastery involves being able to stop the boat and hold it in one place under sail while the crew is occupied with other things. This is at least as important. Knowing that you can manage these things can give a whole new sense of relaxation to your everyday sailing… and it might one day help you to save a life.

The risk

Of all the risks we take at sea, the risk of falling in is the most frequent and the most serious. Jonah will never forget his experience of it, for he was one of the lucky ones who made it back to terra firma. Whales are dying out these days, so there are certain issues about which we need to be quite clear:

■ There is a permanent likelihood of falling overboard. You are just as likely to fall overboard in nice weather as in a gale, but the risks associated with doing so are smaller.

■ Picking up someone lost overboard in good weather is easy, given a certain minimum crew training.

■ In very bad weather, the chances of picking anyone up are slim.

■ At night, whatever the weather, anyone lost overboard cannot be found unless they are equipped with a light.

■ Downwind, by day or night, such accidents are more serious than they are when the boat is close-hauled: you move on past the person in the water very fast, and matters are not made any easier by the fact that you are using a spinnaker or a poled-out genoa.

■ The victim is frequently the skipper, who tends to think that normal rules about clipping on apply only to other people. The crew is often less skilled at carrying out the recovery operation without the skipper's directions to help.

■ This accident can happen to anyone on board, not only those on deck. On one of the Glénans boats, the *Arche*, one crew member was literally extracted from the cabin by a turn in the mainsheet as the boat was gybing, and thrown overboard. On another occasion, aboard the *Glénan*, someone stuck his head out of the cabin to take a bearing just as the boat was knocked flat by a squall: the next minute, he was picking himself out of the guardrail where the sudden knockdown had thrown him. And we all know someone who is so prone to seasickness that they have the habit of rushing out of the cabin on a rough day with neither safety line nor lifejacket on...

■ Falling overboard is by definition unexpected, and often caused by the stupidest things. You can predict sudden broaches or the occasional big wave, but there are always unexpected variations in boat speed, false moves made with a paddle or a boathook, over-anxious grabs after a slippery fish, bailing buckets which pull you off balance, and so on.

■ You can easily fall overboard while the boat is at anchor. This can be very serious if you are anchored in a current, for instance.

Let's face it, having human beings sailing the seas always involves some risk, and you can never make an exhaustive list of the cases in which an accident might happen. For the same reason, there is no known anti-accident panacea. There will always be some new situation which involves you taking a fast decision, on your own: you need to be ready and aware of this.

We should not overdramatise the need for quick decisions: you can avoid much of the risk and much of the need for decisions by taking a few simple precautions. We shall begin by looking at various sorts of precaution, then continue with a look at what to do if an accident happens despite your precautions.

Precautions

Since the beginning of seafaring, people have applied their industry and imagination to the dangers of the sea and invented means for avoiding or minimising the dangers one by one.

There is an enormous range of safety gear available today. Let us run through it quickly in a logical order:

■ the boat's deck has a non-slip finish;

■ if our would-be swimmer slips despite the non-slip surface, there is a toerail and a handrail to grab on to;

■ having missed the handrail, the swimmer next has to overcome the obstacle of the guardrail or the pulpit;

■ once the swimmer has vaulted the safety lines, their own harness line clipped to the jackstay comes into play and holds them fast against the side of the boat;

■ if the harness line breaks (or was not attached in the first place, more likely!), then the swimmer will thank their lucky stars for their lifejacket (if they are wearing one);

■ the orange smoke flare is the next thing into the water, attached to a long line, at the other end of which is the horseshoe lifebuoy. The lifebuoy will keep the swimmer afloat while the boat turns round and comes back;

■ the spot at which the person was lost overboard is marked by a danbuoy;

■ the swimmer should be equipped with a watertight light, an inflatable buoy and a whistle; there should also be reflective strips stuck to everyone's waterproofs, lifejackets and hats, so as to aid recognition in the water (this is one of those rare times in life where you might be thankful for a garish taste in clothes);

■ once the swimmer has been spotted and has a firm grip on a rope or some part of the boat, you must use anything available to get them on board: ladders, ropes, the tender;

■ anyone who has spent a while in the water can be in a sorry state by the time they are back on board: you then need to go through a routine of resuscitation and warming them up to get them back on their (hopefully non-slip) feet.

In listing these precautions, we make two logical assumptions which are actually the opposite of what we would like to believe, namely: that the person was perhaps not clipped on to the boat, and was perhaps not wearing a lifejacket. These are the psychological links in what is otherwise a perfectly logical chain.

This is actually the heart of the problem: if you are clipped on, you have little to worry about; if you are not clipped on, you should be worrying; and if you are short of buoyancy, expect the worst...

When should I clip on and put on my lifejacket?

At what stage does the precaution of clipping your safety harness on become worth while? We have gone through a number of situations above in which clipping on seems to us absolutely imperative. In general, though, this must be left above all to the skipper's judgement. The question the skipper should have constantly in mind is: 'If someone were to fall in the water now, could we rescue them easily?'. If so, fine. If not, harnesses and lifejackets must be worn and used. If either the crew is inexperienced or the boat is unfamiliar to them, the skipper should have a further question in mind: 'If I fell in now, could this bunch rescue me?'. If not, the skipper should be clipped on even in the most perfect conditions.

■ The moral is: you need to take extra precautions not because the risk of falling in has increased, but because the chances of being rescued if you do fall in have decreased.

Recovery manoeuvres

Let us now assume that our Jonah has fallen overboard; despite all our warnings above, he didn't clip on, and his life now depends upon our reactions and the crew's skill.

There are as many correct recovery manoeuvres as there are potential precautions. If the first option fails, the second should be there ready to take its place, and a third after that. If that fails, start again from the beginning. Nor is there a general rule of what you need to do: we shall propose a few courses of action which have been found effective over the years, but we would be the last to claim that our list is exclusive. What you do depends equally on external circumstances, on your crew and your boat. However, there should at least be an agreed procedure for your boat, and everyone on board must know what it is, they must have practised it and they must know what to do in all foreseeable situations, including knowing who takes over if the skipper falls overboard.

The first moments
The first few seconds are vital. Immediately (and preferably simultaneously), the following things must happen:
1   shout *'Man overboard!'* to alert the whole crew;
2   try to *maintain contact* with Jonah by throwing him the orange smoke flare, with the line running out behind it;
3   drop the danbuoy over to mark the spot;
4   *stop the boat* as close as possible to Jonah.
The first three actions are easy, and should be automatic reflexes. Stopping the boat is not always that simple.

Let us look at a few scenarios:
■ The boat is sailing along under normal sail. Whatever point of sailing you are on, the helm can stop the boat by throwing it past head to wind without touching the sheets. This gives you time to think.
■ The boat is under sails which make manoeuvring difficult: a spinnaker or poled-out genoa. You still have to stop. The helm luffs up and lets off the spinnaker guy completely. (This shows the importance of not tying a figure-of-eight knot in the end of the spinnaker sheets: you might need to get rid of the spinnaker completely, letting go the guy, sheet and halyard.) If you are using a poled-out genoa, you luff until the genoa collapses.

The line should be held above the head so you are not towed under the water.

Clearly, the crew will need to practise these manoeuvres to find out how the boat responds to such treatment.

■ The boat was in the middle of some manoeuvre, reefing, changing sails, hoisting or dropping the spinnaker or gybing. (This is a common time to lose someone overboard.) Everyone will be on deck anyway, so you can respond quickly, and you can decide which way to go depending on circumstances.

In many cases, Jonah will be able to grab the orange smoke flare with a short swim of 10 or 20m. He then slips his hand through the loop in the line (or better still, clips his harness on to the loop). When he has done this, those on board make two round turns and two half-hitches with their end of the line around the stern pulpit. It does not matter how much of a mess the jib or spinnaker is in: you have a line to Jonah, and that is the important thing.

With a trained crew, you can get a solid line to the person in the water in the first few seconds in 50 per cent of cases.

If not, you have a few decisions to take, depending on whether you were able to stop the boat or not.

If you can stop

If you were able to stop before all the line was fed out, but you threw the flare too late for Jonah to catch it, then the situation is by no means lost: you have time to get everyone on deck and prepare the boat for the return to the scene of the accident.

While you are waiting:

■ the most important thing is to keep Jonah in sight. If you dropped the danbuoy, there is no immediate risk; otherwise, one person should take on exclusively the job of lookout, announcing that that is what they are doing;

■ and there is an urgent decision to be taken regarding the floating line: whether to pull it in or leave it trailing?

■ It should be pulled in if the weather is good and there is plenty of daylight, as the boat will be turning round quickly anyway. As you approach Jonah, you will need the line again to reach him.

■ It should also be pulled in if the danbuoy is floating visibly and close to Jonah.

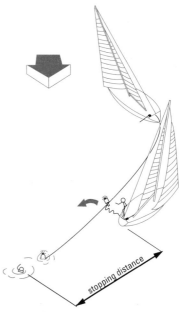

With an orange smoke flare which is properly installed and easy to throw, it is easy to make up for the stopping distance of the boat.

■

Stopping at all costs

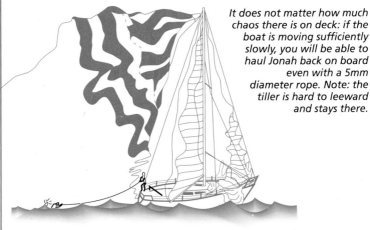

It does not matter how much chaos there is on deck: if the boat is moving sufficiently slowly, you will be able to haul Jonah back on board even with a 5mm diameter rope. Note: the tiller is hard to leeward and stays there.

In gentle weather, even under spinnaker, Jonah will be able to catch the floating flare without you throwing all the line overboard. The only change you need to make to the sails is to let out the spinnaker guy.

If there are not enough of you to drop the spinnaker, you just need to let off the halyard and sheet to get rid of it. The spinnaker is comparatively worthless anyway.

It must be left trailing if you have a second line, if it is night, if the danbuoy light is not working, in bad conditions or if it will take you a while to turn the boat round. Under these circumstances, the floating flare is actually a useful marker for the place you lost touch, and can be a good place to meet up again. Be careful, though: it is hard to keep the flare in one place if you heave to and tack round, as you will inevitably drag the flare downwind as you make leeway. Someone must control the line by hand, preferably from the leeward bow. One member of the crew makes a note of the bearing from the buoy to the last seen position of the person in the water.

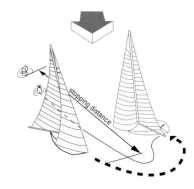

With a sufficiently long line, and if the boat can stop before all the line has gone out, Jonah will have time to swim to the flare. A well-trained crew on a properly equipped boat can get a solid line to the person in the water, in most cases in half a minute.

If you cannot stop

If you cannot stop the boat before all the flare line is in the water, the boat and flare are continuing to sail away from Jonah and the crew will most likely lose sight of him, especially if there is no danbuoy or it does not work. This is a critical situation, and it will become a desperate one if you do not take appropriate measures immediately.

1 *Dropping a buoy as close as possible to Jonah*, if you have not already done so, should be your first action. You note down his position by reference to the buoy and start the *emergency navigation.*

2 *Start a zigzag back*, preferably with the wind just ahead of the beam, such that your zigzag course will bring you past Jonah's last known location. You will find that this is also the point of sailing on which the boat is easiest to control.

3 *Alert other shipping* as soon as you are on the beam reach and have started your emergency navigation. Use any means at your disposal: rocket flares if there are other boats in sight, VHF radio on band 16 or single side band at 2182 KHz. This is entirely justified by the situation.

Spotting the man overboard

If Jonah or the danbuoy are in view, sail back towards them; if not, follow the directions of the emergency navigator.

Dropping a buoy is so important we cannot stress it sufficiently. The only way this emergency can become fatal is if you fail to find the person in the water. Doubtless some people have drowned fairly soon after falling overboard, but how many more must there be who

115

have been perfectly conscious, watching their boat criss-crossing a route leading gradually further away? A person in the water with no lifejacket has a chance of being seen as much as 100m away, but you need to be less than 50m away to be sure of spotting them. This illustrates how precise your emergency navigation needs to be and how important it is to drop a marker right at the spot of the mishap: the marker is the only way you can be sure of finding Jonah again.

If Jonah is not found again immediately, you have to start combing the area.

Search patterns

Searching an area means crossing it back and forth so that you go within a maximum of 50m of every point in the area at least twice. We recommend the following method: take two points about 200m to windward and to leeward of the estimated location of the fall, and tack from one to the other. Each tack should be 100m long, i.e. take about a minute in the average boat, including tacks. You then extend the area to be searched by another 200m to leeward and to windward, making your tacks 200–300m long, say, two minutes including the turn. The tacks should be less close to the wind than usual so your zigzags do not take you more than 50m from any point in the area. You can mark the area to be searched with floating objects (for instance fenders) which are equipped with sea anchors (such as buckets, coils of rope, lightly weighted clothes…) so they do not drift too far.

But are you searching the right area? This is the harrowing question everyone asks themselves, especially if they failed to put out markers on the spot in time. While the boat is searching back and forth, one crew member should systematically check the emergency navigator's calculations.

The search must continue while there is still a chance of finding Jonah alive. In the Atlantic, in temperate latitudes, you should not give up searching for a person in a lifejacket for eight to ten hours.

What if I am Jonah?

You do not just lie back waiting to be rescued. You can contribute to your own rescue.

The first thing to do is to try and catch hold of the line if it is within reach. You should not attempt to swim long distances, because this could be exhausting, and you might be in the water for some time. Of course, if you are not wearing a lifejacket, it is worth trying a little harder to reach the line, because there is a lifebuoy on the end, which can give you much-needed buoyancy.

As soon as you have hold of the line, or have worked out that you will not be able to get hold of it, you need to improve your flotation, if necessary by blowing up your lifejacket or getting into the lifebuoy.

HELP (Heat Escape Lessening Position), which gives the slowest possible rate of heat loss.

You also need to check and adjust your harness fitting.

The next thing to do is to ensure that you lose heat at the slowest possible rate, by closing all zips (and keeping your boots on), reducing movement to a minimum and taking up the HELP position if possible.

You should make yourself as visible as possible using your bright hood, inflatable day marker ball, shining your torch at night, and whistling when rescuers are nearby. Finally be prepared mentally to watch them sail by without seeing you.

Establishing a line

Once Jonah has been found, he needs to be attached to the boat quickly, easily and precisely. While a boat is reaching it can sail quickly, and steering becomes more precise at speed. The boat should pass close to Jonah (3 to 5m away) and the floating flare should be thrown 2 to 3m in front of him so as not to knock him out. The boat then continues for another two or three boat lengths before tacking and heaving to without letting go the sheets.

Is it better to pass to windward or to leeward? It does not matter much, so long as you pass close. Nevertheless, it is easier to throw downwind than upwind…

If you miss Jonah, start again in the same way, but leaving a little more space and time. This is a case where more haste means less speed: you need to remain calm and overcome the anxiety and worry which inevitably influence everyone's behaviour in this situation.

If you left the line floating and were lucky enough to have Jonah catch it, then you can pull the line along forward and 20cm below the surface of the water using the boathook. The boat should be stopped as soon as there is a line established to Jonah.

If you have more than one line on board, you can attach a small float to a warp approximately 20 or 30m long, with a loop on the end.

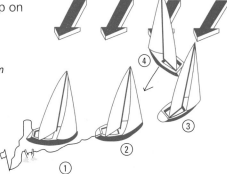

1 Pass close to Jonah on a beam reach and throw the line.
2 Continue on the same course for two or three boat lengths.
3 Tack, but do not release the jib.
4 Drift back hove to towards Jonah.

117

If the search took a long time or Jonah seems exhausted, and espe-cially if he is not wearing lifejacket or harness, a crew member, warmly dressed, fully equipped and firmly attached to the boat, should jump in and take hold of Jonah around the middle to keep him buoyed up. As soon as possible, another line should be made fast: you do not want to risk losing the person you have just rescued. Any line used should be kept loose and with a little 'give' in it. To avoid sudden jolts, the lines should be hand-held by someone on deck; and to avoid acci-dents, they should also be secured to a cleat, leaving a little slack.

What about the engine?

We have so far limited our description of the search to using the sails. However, the engine can be of great assistance in this exercise. No one cares about style: it's results that count, and just as you need to be able to use the sails in case of engine failure, you need to be able to use the engine in case the sails will not work.

On a sailing vessel, you are probably under sail when Jonah falls overboard; so we have assumed that recovery manoeuvres at least be-gin under sail. Once you have dropped a marker buoy or established his position, and got the boat and the emergency navigation sorted out, you can think about continuing the operation under engine power.

If the engine is to be used, it must be sufficiently powerful to allow you to manoeuvre exactly as you need in the prevailing conditions, the sails must be dropped and stowed; and all trailing ropes which might get in the way of the propeller must be brought inboard.

A mixture of sails and engine is not recommended, as there is too great a danger of catching a rope in the propeller.

If you manage to fulfil all these conditions, retrieving your lost crew member could well be easier under engine power than with the sails. There are still problems, though: the rescue line in particular, and Jonah, whom we do not wish to injure as we come to collect him!

If the weather is really awful, some sailing boats will not be able to turn their bow through the wind, in which case they have to be turned stern to wind. This inevitably means losing ground to windward, so the engine should be used in reverse until you are facing dead downwind; you follow this by luffing up as fast as possible, with the engine full speed ahead and the tiller right down to leeward.

Bringing Jonah aboard

How is Jonah feeling at this point? Let us ask him. 'Thou didst cast me into the deep, into the heart of the seas, and the flood was round about me, all thy waves and billows passed over me.' More than a little shaken, in other words. This is not the time for pleasantries. The most difficult part of the operation is probably still before you.

Of course occasionally you will have a couple of gorillas on board who can pull their shipmate out of the drink straight away, and he'll be right as rain. This is the exception. Basically, even in pleasant weather, the person who falls overboard falls into another world: paralysed by fear and stricken by a panic attack, even the soberest individual cannot be immune. There is no training session which can prepare you for the real thing: every natural instinct actually works against a quick and efficient rescue, as you

Jonah to leeward, boat hove to. This is the best starting point for bringing your pal back on board.

clamp your fingers white-knuckled to the nearest rail, and your gallant rescuers may well have to unclamp them for you, forcibly. A moment later every ounce of strength ebbs away and you would fall back into the water unless you were firmly held. Add to that your weight: you may weigh only 75kg dry, but a suit full of water can make that up to 110–120, and any heeling of the boat can add enough momentum to make your rescuers feel as though they are lifting 200kg. If you are not wearing a harness, it will be difficult to get hold of you, especially in rough weather. To pull such a difficult lump aboard, your rescuers need to know what they are doing; they need the correct gear; and they need to have practised.

Bringing Jonah alongside

Once Jonah is attached to the boat by a line, he needs to be brought round to a spot from which he can be hoisted aboard. On a monohull, this spot is slightly aft of the mast and to leeward. This is where the boat has least freeboard, and even that can be reduced by heeling the boat; you are also sheltered from the worst of the waves, and drifting slightly downwind, thus keeping Jonah firmly alongside. There are two problems with this: it is occasionally difficult to get Jonah in place; and once there, he may be so well pushed up against the hull that he can be washed under it. If the boat has a transom scoop, Jonah can be manoeuvred into that and hoisted up, though any pitching of the boat

Any method which works is acceptable... but some are more effective than others.

in the sea can render this operation most dangerous. Multihulls have such narrow hulls that Jonah should be brought on board wherever there is room for the rescuers: in this case, freeboard is a secondary consideration.

Unfortunately, the likeliest place for Jonah to end up is behind the boat and to windward, and *it is to avoid this that we tack and heave to, several boat lengths after we have passed the line to him.*

If you do this and then pull the line from the foredeck, Jonah will arrive naturally at the right spot. If he is behind the boat and to windward, you can pull him all the way round the stern, so long as there is someone in the water with him to help him fend the boat off, or he is capable of doing this himself; alternatively, you can tack round, giving the line a certain amount of slack as you do so, but not letting go. This is rather easier under engine than under sail.

Hoisting Jonah aboard

You should now waste no time in pulling Jonah aboard, as experience shows that it is difficult to keep him in the right place for long.

On a small boat with little free-board, the operation is fairly simple: the boat is hove to and heeling slightly, with the weight of the crew to leeward accentuating the heel. The rail is thus at about water level, and you only need to undo or cut the lower safety

Pull him alongside then roll him to a convenient spot...

wire for Jonah to be dragged on board. There is no real hoisting involved: he rolls into the boat as one might roll a sack of potatoes.

If there is a little too much freeboard for you to do this, you

... for two of you to grab him under the armpits.

might be able to drag Jonah out of the water by seizing him under the armpits. If you do this, he should be facing away from the boat, or his knees will catch on the way up.

On a large boat with lots of free-board or a multihull the operation is quite different. The first solution that comes to mind is the boarding ladder. If this is to be used it must be up to the job: it should be rigid and solidly attached to the transom, with at least three rungs going down below the water surface. If Jonah has the strength to grab on and climb up, then the problem is solved; and this is the case sufficiently often to justify the presence of the ladder. If Jonah is too exhausted to climb the ladder, the situation is entirely different, depending on whether he is wearing a harness (with a crotch strap, of course) or not.

Assuming Jonah is wearing a harness and has been able to hook on to a line, you are in no further danger of losing each other. So

Use a specially rigged block and tackle on a halyard end…

long as the hook holds, it is a question of strength, and a sufficiently well rigged block and tackle should be able to hoist a giant aboard without needing too much strength.

If Jonah has no harness on, you are still not on the home straight. There are appalling instances of boats managing to bring a crew member alongside, only to find their efforts to hoist them aboard ending by pulling their clothing off piece by piece, while the person stays firmly in the water. Depending on the circumstances, it may be appropriate to send a correctly harnessed crew member overboard to help, or to use the tender or the liferaft. If you use the liferaft, be very careful with its painter and fixing points, which were not designed for this sort of use.

… or even the inflatable dinghy.

First aid

You have brought your shipmate back on board. If he is still in good shape, celebration all round. Occasionally, though, he will be less than fully fit. If he is just generally frozen, it is still relatively simple. It would be a terrible shame to have got this far and then to lose the battle… so on we go.

Warmth

If anyone has spent a considerable length of time in the water getting hypothermic, even if they did not lose consciousness, they need to be warmed up. This must not happen just anyhow. The usual techniques one hears about – undressing the person, rubbing them or giving them a draught of scotch – are not only useless, they can actually do harm.

When the body cools down, a number of reactions take place to restrict the blood flow. Firstly, the blood vessels around the outer parts (or peripheral zone) of the body constrict, then those a little closer in (the intermediate zone), leaving blood flowing properly only around the vital organs such as the heart and brain and keeping these warm. If the vital organs begin to cool down even by tenths of a degree, things can become fatal.

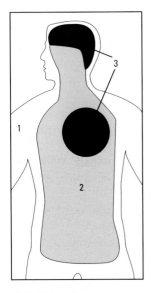

1 Peripheral zone
2 Intermediate zone
3 Vital organs

When someone has been badly exposed to the cold, the first step to take is to avoid any further reduction in body temperature. They should not be undressed, but insulated from the outside air by being put in a big plastic sack and pressed close between two or three other people. (A sleeping bag will do if there is no survival bag on board.) The person should not be rubbed, nor given alcohol to drink. Both of these would dilate the blood vessels at the outer edges of the body, causing blood to rush to the outside while it is still relatively cold. This cooled blood would return to the vital organs and drastically lower the core temperature.

Giving hot drinks to anyone who has been pulled out of the sea is acceptable, as this warms them from the inside. If you cannot warm the person quickly, you should head for land and the nearest doctor as soon as possible.

Resuscitation

If Jonah is unconscious, there are two possible reasons:

■ asphyxia due to swallowing too much water, which might leave him no longer breathing for the moment, but with his heart still beating;

■ immersion syncope, which is a sudden loss of consciousness due to the difference in temperature between the body and the surrounding water, with loss of heartbeat, followed (if the body is still in the water) by asphyxia.

Once he is back on board, you need to check that his heart is still beating, and at the same time start artificial respiration. The best place to find a pulse is not on the wrist, but inside the groin, on the femoral artery. If there is no heartbeat, you need to carry out heart resuscitation at the same time as getting him breathing.

Mouth-to-mouth

Believe us, the slightest loss of time can mean disaster. Now is not the time to teach yourself mouth-to-mouth resuscitation. You need to have attended a course, learnt and practised it previously, and carried out exercises using a dummy. If any crew members have not been through such a course, it is by no means ridiculous for the skipper to carry out a training session before setting out from harbour on the first day.

Mouth-to-mouth resuscitation is carried out as follows:

■ The patient is laid out flat on their back, with their head facing to one side to ensure they do not swallow their tongue, and to remove dentures, spittle or any foreign bodies. This must be done very quickly.

■ The head is taken in both hands and stretched well back. This is essential: the patient's throat should be stretched so that the air can get into their lungs. (It is useful to put a pile of clothes under their shoulders.)

■ Press with one hand on the patient's forehead. With one hooked finger of the other hand, pull their lower lip down so as to open their mouth wide.

■ Press your lips close around the patient's mouth, pressing your cheek against their nostrils to avoid air escaping that way.

■ Blow hard. You should see their chest rise. If it does not, this is probably because the head is not far enough back.

■ Draw back slightly to let them breathe out, then blow again according to whatever rhythm suits you (about 12–15 cycles per minute).

The patient's head needs to be put well back so as to open the top of the windpipe, or no air will be able to pass.

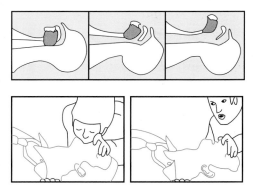

A few special cases:

■ if the patient is rigid and you cannot open their mouth, you have to use mouth-to-nose. The head position is the same; use one hand to press their forehead back and down; use the thumb of the other to keep their lips closed. Blow, but be careful not to obstruct the nasal passages. Part the patient's lips to help them breathe out, then start the cycle again;

■ if the patient is a child, put your lips over mouth and nose together. Stop blowing as soon as the chest inflates and blow in a faster rhythm than for adults (about 20 cycles per minute);

■ there are special tubes available (Douglas Airways) for artificial respiration, which are particularly useful for preventing the patient's tongue falling back.

Pinch the patient's nose shut and press your mouth against the patient's. Let the air escape naturally, then start again, with about 12 to 15 breathing cycles per minute.

■

Man overboard drill

The purpose of drilling is so that the reflexes which could save your ship-mate's life become second nature. You should drill as often as possible without letting the drill become monotonous.

There are three phases to the man overboard drill:
1 Throwing the line and the danbuoy over.
2 Getting into position for the pickup.
3 Bringing Jonah on board.
The exercises can be broken down further.

1 Throwing the heaving line

The purpose of practising this is that the crew should learn the fastest way to the floating flare and heaving line, and learn about their surroundings, so they know which direction it is easiest to throw in and where one can throw the line so as not to tangle it in the rigging. You can practice this en route, throwing at no particular target to start with, then maybe aiming at a lobster pot buoy. It is preferable for the skipper to order: 'Jim, throw the heaving line at the pot!' rather than 'Man overboard!' when practising this part of the drill. Once every member of the crew has practised throwing the heaving line out three or four times it is worth while proceeding to a fuller drill.

2 Positioning yourself for the pickup

You need a dummy for this exercise: anything that floats, such as a life-jacket, weighted down with a sea anchor such as a bucket, and with a 4 to 5m line attached which has a lump of wood or cork on the end. The exercise consists of dropping the line less than 4 to 5m from the dummy, then stopping the boat before you reach the end of the line. Once the practice session is over, the dummy can be picked up by catching the boathook under the floating line.

3 Bringing Jonah on board

This is an important exercise. It does not matter how quickly you can find and get a line to a crew member in a force 10: if you cannot bring them on board, they will not survive.

The exercise really only has validity if you have a crew member to play dead, lying in the bottom of the tender. It should be carried out with and without harness.

You will quickly realise that a Jonah with no lifejacket needs a rope tied around his chest if he is not to be lost. You will also notice that it becomes very difficult to lift a limp body.

Note: it is considerably easier to hoist a dry and comfortable person feigning unconsciousness than it is to bring a wet and scared (or worse still, panic-stricken) Jonah on board.

Cardiac resuscitation

If the patient's heart has stopped, you need to restart it at the same time as carrying out mouth-to-mouth resuscitation. If you are carrying out the operation alone, you carry out five cardiac massages between each breathing cycle, as follows:

■ place the heel of your left hand on the lower third of the breastbone, *in the middle* of the chest, and place your right hand on your left;

■ with your arms straight, press down with all your weight on the breastbone. Make a series of short, sharp pushes in groups of two.

If the patient is old or a child, you should avoid pressing too hard or you might break one of their ribs. The massage is then better carried out one-handed; for very small children, use just two fingers.

Mouth-to-mouth resuscitation and cardiac massages need to be carried out with the same commitment and perseverance as any of the preceding operations. You must not give up hope: 'drowned men' have been known to open their eyes after six hours of no apparent success. If there are several of you, keep going in relays until you see some sign of life.

Afterwards, it is best to visit a doctor as soon as possible with the newly revived patient.

Summary

All of the operations described in this chapter are standard ones, requiring standard, cheap, reliable and simple equipment: a heaving line, a danbuoy and a block and tackle. All three items have a right to be on board any boat, and you must practise their use. The drills we suggest are easy to carry out and will not disturb your cruising even on the calmest of days.

Bringing a member of the crew back on board when they have fallen over the side in the daytime, in pleasant weather, is a simple operation for a trained crew. A trained crew also has a good chance of success in carrying out the same operation in bad weather.

But if a member of a poorly trained crew falls overboard with no lifejacket and no harness on, they do not stand a chance, whatever the weather.

There is no harm in admitting it: some of us are here to tell the tale today because we were fortunate enough to be fished out quickly after nasty accidents; some of us have helped others out of difficulty; and all of us are the heirs to a strong tradition of safe sailing in the Glénans school. Over the thousands of miles covered by members of our community, the number of accidents has been astonishingly small, and this testifies to the traditions of safety. Alas, even at les Glénans, the number is not zero, however.

In case we have not made ourselves clear enough already, let us just repeat once more:

I PRACTISE
I ENCOURAGE OTHERS TO PRACTISE
WE PRACTISE TOGETHER.